Breaking the Cycle

Gender, Literacy, and Learning

EDITED BY
Lynne B. Alvine
Linda E. Cullum

Boynton/Cook Publishers
HEINEMANN
Portsmouth, NH

Boynton/Cook Publishers, Inc.
A subsidiary of Reed Elsevier Inc.
361 Hanover Street
Portsmouth, NH 03801–3912
http://www.boyntoncook.com

Offices and agents throughout the world

The author and publisher wish to thank those who have generously given permission to reprint borrowed material: "Plastic Princess" by Stephanie Anderson originally appeared in *Writing Takes You Everywhere*. Published by the Pennsylvania Writing and Literature Project, August, 1997. Reprinted by permission.

Library of Congress Cataloging-in-Publication Data
Breaking the cycle : gender, literacy, and learning / edited by
  Lynne B. Alvine, Linda E. Cullum.
      p.   cm.
    Includes bibliographical references.
    ISBN 0-86709-490-7
    1. English language—Study and teaching (Secondary)—United States—
Sex differences.   2. Reading comprehension—United States—Sex
differences.   3. Women—Education—United States.   4. Sex differences
in education—United States.   I. Alvine, Lynne B.   II. Cullum, Linda E.
LB1631.B764   1999
428.4'071'2—dc21   99-15379
                                                                                        CIP

Editor: Lisa Luedeke
Production: Elizabeth Valway
Cover design: Jenny Jensen Greenleaf
Cover photo: Barbara Eidel
Manufacturing: Louise Richardson

Printed in the United States of America on acid-free paper
03 02 01 00 99 DA 1 2 3 4 5

Contents

Foreword

At a recent meeting of the Class V Mother Daughter Book Club at my new school, we were discussing Katherine Paterson's *The Flip Flop Girl*. I was glad to hear the girls speaking with such conviction about the women in the story: the mother, the grandmother, and the two adolescent girl characters. I smiled to myself at their lack of inhibition, their eagerness to share their opinions, and their shimmering confidence. Fifth graders are fantastic, I thought to myself, as my eyes caught those of Kelly Herrity, their teacher. You are doing a great job with them, I told her silently.

Then, all of a sudden, the conversation turned. Emily was talking about her grandmother's funeral and about how she had felt seeing her in the casket. Tears streamed down her face as she shared this memory with us. Kelly and I have been part of enough literature groups and writing groups to know that such a show of emotion is par for the course, a tribute to the book and a sign that there is mutual trust among the people gathered. However, some of the moms in the room seemed a little nonplussed. I pushed on, asking the girls about another aspect of the book—the difficulty of being a new girl in school, moving to a new place, having left friends and familiar settings behind. More tears, this time from Jackie, who had just come to our school a few weeks earlier. Tissues, sniffles, a few awkward giggles, and we carried on.

Later one of the mothers, after telling me how much she had enjoyed the group, said, "Mrs. Barbieri, next time, a cheerier book?" Taken aback, I replied, "Well, some of the best books do deal with some of the most difficult situations. It's important for girls to have a chance to read about these." She nodded and expressed her trust in my judgment. I thought of Katherine Paterson's belief that stories must "articulate the glorious but fragile human condition for those whose hearts have heard but whose mouths, at the age of five or ten or fourteen, can't yet express . . . to communicate that which lies in our deepest heart, which has no words, which can only be hinted at through the means of a story" (1990). I thought of the girls themselves, the girls I have known and been privileged to work with over the past fifteen years. I thought of my Friday's Feisty Females in Chinatown; I thought of the Cleveland girls at Laurel School and the South Carolina girls I taught when we lived down there. These were all girls who struggled to be known, to be validated in what they knew, to be seen and heard and recognized, and, most of all, to have relationships with others. These were all girls who needed stories that would shake their hearts and call forth in them insight, compassion, and empathy.

The Feisties, as we eventually called ourselves, were eighth graders, most of them new immigrants from China. We read books and poems, and kept writers' notebooks. It was in these notebooks that the girls were able to jot down their observations of the city, as we hopped the subway every Friday to visit museums, parks, or restaurants. Often they would write about their memories of China, and I came to see the notebooks as precious reliquaries, holding places for lost dreams and blueprints for future lives. They used their notebooks to ask questions, too, to wonder about their new identities as Americans, their roles as young adult women in a new culture. Sophia worried that the way she dressed might preclude her acceptance into the "cool group" at school. On the other hand, she insisted that she wanted to create art "that says who I am, not what somebody thinks I should be." Catherine wrote about her yearning to know more, do more, and become more, all the while lamenting myriad perceived inadequacies. "I have so much pain in me," she wrote. "You don't know. It is very deep in me."

Issues of popularity and self-worth loomed large in the lives of my students in Ohio and South Carolina, too. How can a girl assert her individuality, her convictions, based on what she knows to be true, and at the same time build and maintain connections to other people? A perpetual and universal dilemma for young girls, it is one that we discovered could be examined deeply and richly through careful reading of books like Paterson's *The Flip Flop Girl*, Bette Greene's *The Drowning of Stephan Jones*, Karin Cook's *What Girls Know*, and Jean Staples' *Shabanu*—with open, honest, sometimes painful discussions—and through writing, particularly in writers' notebooks.

What has been crucial in each context has been this meaningful immersion into literacy: reading, writing, listening, and talking. Our girls need to be supported in their struggle to hold onto what they know—it is tragic to lose a grandma; it hurts like the devil to leave friends and have to start all over again at a new school—as they negotiate the complex demands of a materialistic culture that sends them mixed messages. They need to read about other girls' struggles; they need to write about their own. And they need to work with adult women in small-group settings to talk about their reactions to books and to the world and to be reassured that they are not in this alone.

Lynne Alvine, Linda Cullum, and the other authors in this beautiful new collection, *Breaking the Cycle: Gender, Literacy, and Learning*, offer new testament to the wonder of literacy and the power of women mentoring girls. The careful research, heartrending stories, and comprehensive resource lists they present will be invaluable to teachers, parents, and girls themselves. They offer a panoply of ways to use literacy, from teaching critical theory to exploring the world of teen zines. And these teacher-authors are always right there, on the front lines, walking shoulder to shoulder with their students, nudging them forward in their quests to examine choices; to be who they are; and to make the world better for all women, and, consequently, for all humankind. As a teacher, a mother, and a woman, I am greatly heartened by their work, which offers new light and hope for our students, our daughters, and ourselves.

Maureen Barbieri
Head of Middle School
Marymount School
New York, NY

Reference

Paterson, K. 1990. "Heart in Hiding." In *Worlds of Childhood: The Art and Craft of Writing for Children*, ed. by W. Zinsser. Boston: Houghton Mifflin.

PART I

The Concerns

As the river of a girl's life flows into the sea of Western culture, she is in danger of drowning or disappearing. To take on the problem of appearance, which is the problem of her development, and to connect her life with history on a cultural scale, she must enter—and by entering disrupt—a tradition in which "human" has for the most part meant male. Thus a struggle often breaks out in girls' lives at the edge of adolescence, and the fate of this struggle becomes key to girls' development and to Western civilization.
—CAROL GILLIGAN, "Prologue," *Making Connections*

1

Learning to Break the Cycle

LYNNE B. ALVINE AND LINDA E. CULLUM

As a ninth grader, Amy[1] proudly completed her first children's book, a multicultural fairy tale that would later be bound, illustrated, and displayed as a fine example of what literacy can produce. But literacy can also reproduce; it can be used to reproduce cultural images of what it means to be male and female in our society. What are those images? Amy's story flashes some of them before us.

MARGARITA THE MEXICAN JUMPING BEAN

It was a hot dusty morning in San Guapo. Margarita was awakened suddenly when her bean started to roll down the street. Margarita was a caterpillar who lived in a Mexican jumping bean. Caterpillars are what make the beans jump. Every day Margarita would eat away pieces of the bean to try to get out. Sometimes she would bounce against the sides of the bean to try to shatter it.

Margarita was tired of being alone. She wanted friends, to get out of her bean, to see the world! One day, Pepe the roadrunner came to San Guapo. While walking down the street he saw the bean hopping all around. He heard Margarita crying and exclaimed "Hey bean, why are you crying?"

"I'm not a bean," Margarita cried. "I'm a caterpillar trapped inside!"

"How can I help?" asked Pepe. "I'll crack the bean with my beak."

"No, there's no use! I'm trapped forever," cried Margarita.

"I'm not going to let you give up," yelled Pepe as he pecked the bean right in half!

"Oh my," Margarita screamed as she rolled out on the ground.

"Thank you so much! What is your name?"

3

"Pepe, the roadrunner, and yours?"

"Margarita is my name, and I'm free! Thank you so much Pepe! You have found a friend for life!"

"Well then, let me be the first to show you the world," exclaimed Pepe as he helped her gather her belongings. So with that he hoisted her up on his back, and they spent the rest of their lives enjoying the world and each other.

THE END

Margarita, the female title character, struggles to be in control of her own fate, but fails until Pepe, her hero, comes along. He sets her "free" to spend the rest of her life carried on his back.

Amy has learned her lessons well. She has learned the "appropriate" behaviors for her male and female characters, Pepe and Margarita. She also has learned that it is okay, even "natural," for girls to love reading and writing. Yet the stories that Amy will read and write, like the stories of millions of other girls, are typically not her own. Amy has subconsciously demonstrated Judith Fetterly's assertion (1978) that girls' stories will be of a "man's world," a world they inevitably come to recognize as universal, yet distinctly not female.

Young men also suffer from this literacy bifurcation. For while they may readily recognize and validate their experiences in the pages of books, and may have stories like Amy's to tell, for them to enjoy reading and writing is often stigmatized. For boys, literacy practices are easily dismissed as "girl stuff" in favor of playing sports and video games, appropriate training for the marketplace and for the combat zone.

The irony hardly needs to be stated. Literacy has the unique potential for expanding all students' understanding of their personal worlds and those of others around them. Too often, however, reading and writing constrain the development of both girls and boys—by reifying, rather than disrupting, definitions of what it means to be "female" or "male" in a patriarchal culture. The need for disrupting those definitions is most crucial at the time when the culture's lessons are most readily absorbed, during the adolescent years. It is then that young people are struggling with their changing bodies, their burgeoning sexuality, their fragile sense of self and other, and, perhaps above all, their desperate and often frustrating need to understand themselves in terms of the larger cultural scheme of things.

As English language arts teachers, it is our responsibility—and our privilege—to recognize the ways that literacy learning can help young women and men with this all-consuming project. By becoming aware of the messages our culture sends through reading, writing, and visual representations, students can move beyond cultural assumptions. They can use their emerging literacy to expand rather than to circumscribe their horizons. This awareness is a gift that teachers can give to their students—and to themselves.

To that end, we offer this collection of original essays designed not only to explore the cultural reproduction of gender role stereotypes, but also to offer suggestions for ways teachers can be agents for breaking that cycle of reproduction, especially for the girls in their classrooms. For it is not enough to become aware of the ways that gender role socialization limits the literacy learning of all students. It is also important that teachers have the appropriate materials and practical strategies necessary to help students disrupt the cultural messages they receive—messages that have a direct impact on their reading and writing lives.

What, then, are the concerns? Amy's story offers an excellent example of the powerful cultural messages she had internalized by ninth grade. In Chapter 2, Andrea Fishman offers further evidence of the pervasive nature of cultural imprinting. Stories written by girls responding to a specific prompt at an all-girl parochial school are quite different from stories written by girls in a mixed-gender public middle school. These differences leave little doubt that school culture does, indeed, heavily affect girls' perceptions of what it is to grow up female. If school culture can make such a difference, we must, indeed, concern ourselves with the messages that pervade school climates.

As we explored possibilities for organizing the balance of this collection, we recognized that some of the essays clearly resonated with others. We put those essays together and gave each grouping a thematic label. The collection tends to move from the more general to the more specific, from the global to the particular. If it suits you, read them in that order—or find your own way.

Though the focus of this collection is girls, other researchers have explored specific ways that gender role stereotyping disadvantages adolescent boys. See "Boys—The Understudied Majority" in Chapter 12 for resources on how gender role stereotypes constrain boys' development and self-actualization.

Each of the three essays in Part Two offers a rationale and specific strategies for curricular transformation at the secondary level. In "Reaching and Teaching Girls," Janet Montelaro argues that middle schools would do well to adopt a "women's studies" approach in all subject areas. She calls for nothing short of a complete transformation of content and teaching practices across the middle school curriculum.

Adopting a women's studies approach to curriculum content and pedagogy suggests that we find more appropriate ways to help students value their progress and to report that progress to parents. Many teachers have

experienced the frustration of watching their forward-looking feminist pedagogy clash with institutional expectations for evaluation methods that reflect
a model of teacher-centered authority and competitive ranking. In "Evaluation Brought to Life: Reconceiving Assessment in Classrooms," Kathy Sanford grapples with these issues and offers an effective program of reflection
and self-assessment that she first instituted in an eighth grade all-girl setting.

In "A Net of Relationships: Gender Issues 101," teaching colleagues Alice
Cross and Geraldine O'Neill take a fresh, honest look at their high school's attempts to institute positive curricular change with the introduction of a cross-
disciplinary gender studies course. Their insights into the project's successes,
their understandings of why the course did not become an integral part of the
school curriculum, and their detailed course descriptions could be helpful to
anyone hoping to create a similar cross-disciplinary middle or high school
gender studies course. Cross and O'Neill and their colleagues taught Gender
Issues 101 for only one semester, but they learned a great deal; in sharing their
curriculum development process and their course syllabus, they provide a
guide for others.

The two chapters in Part Three focus specifically on adolescent girls as
readers. Both essays underscore the importance of recognizing the personal
impact of reading on girls' lives and of encouraging girls to take their reading
personally. Deborah Appleman describes her independent study with a high
school girl who asked to learn about "women's studies." Even as Alice pushed
against her own perception of what it is to be a feminist, she learned to read—
and to appreciate reading—with a feminist lens.

Judith Hayn and Lisa Spiegel urge middle and high school English teachers to include more young adult fiction and nonfiction, especially titles with
strong female characters, in middle and high school literature assignments.
These two specialists in adolescent literature review sixty-four titles in "Beyond Anne Frank and Scout: Females in Young Adult Literature." They also
offer a number of specific classroom strategies for using literature to raise
students' consciousness about gender.

Though the limitations that adolescent girls experience in school literacy learning are not unique to any particular social class or racial group, class
and gender differences do come into play. We believe that this collection of
essays includes examples of how those limitations are similar across groups as
well as specific ways they may be different.

Appleman and Fishman offer a window on the literacy learning of
working-class and middle-class adolescents; the two essays in Part Four focus
on specific cultures outside of the mainstream. In "Striking Out: Girl vs. Girl
Culture in an Alternative School," Annemarie Oldfield paints a disturbing

portrait of the process of socialization her adolescent female students undergo at the hands of their female role models. The young women she describes have been systematically encouraged to deny positive regard for both themselves and other females so that they may serve the men in their lives: their fathers, brothers, boyfriends, and even the two-timing, estranged lovers who have fathered their babies.

In "Taking Black Girls Seriously: Addressing Discrimination's Double Bind," Lynn Spradlin offers a theoretical analysis of this often-overlooked segment of our female student population. Focusing specifically on understanding and addressing the phenomenon of "loud black girls," she explains how the dominant culture compels African American female students to identify not with their white counterparts, who at adolescence are retreating into silence and passivity, but with white males. She describes this usually neglected coping strategy of "gender passing" and offers important suggestions for acknowledging our black female students and helping them to discover their own voices.

Oscar Wilde once observed that anything really worth knowing cannot be taught. The relatively recent underground literary phenomenon of "zining" offers support for Wilde's point. Through their zines, adolescents—primarily girls—have made commitments to literacy that reach far beyond those of the educational system with its many conventions. The chapters in Part Five, "Who's at Risk? Entering the World of Adolescent Zines" and "Notes from the Zine Underground," explore this fascinating emergent literacy practice. First, Elizabeth Dutro, Jennifer Sinor, and Sara Rubinow weave together their zine research and excerpts from their own journals to explore the zine community and to caution teachers against the impulse to violate this amazing literacy phenomenon by attempting to institutionalize it. Then, high school junior Kimra McPherson, an active member of the zine community, gives readers an inside glimpse at being a "zinestress." Her essay serves as a testimony to the power of literacy in girls' lives.

Though you will find suggestions for curricular materials and strategies for teaching included throughout this collection of essays, in Chapter 12 Linda Cullum provides an annotated bibliography of over one hundred resources on gender-fair schooling and literacy learning—all written since 1990. Titled "Gender Fare: In Support of Gender Equity in Literacy Learning," the list is both extensive and selective. Perhaps the list itself is a hopeful indication that the cycle is, indeed, being disrupted.

Finally, we end the book with a poem that reflects the potential for the spirit of an adolescent girl or adult woman to be both whole and integrated. Written by our poet friend and colleague Jessica Jopp, "Song of Happiness" speaks something of our wish for the teachers and teacher educators who work to break the cycle of inequity in literacy learning, and for the girls and women who will share the blessings of their work.

Notes

1. Amy is a pseudonym, as are all of the names used in Chapters 2, 4, 6, and 10, which are based on ethnographic studies.

Reference

Fetterly, J. 1978. *The Resisting Reader.* Bloomington: Indiana University Press.

2

Plastic Princesses

Empowering Girls to Break the Mold

ANDREA FISHMAN

Plastic Princess

A little girl looked at Barbie,
With her shining golden hair,
And said, "I want to look like her.
Only about looks now I care."

How I pity this little girl,
With the brain and very modest.
She would've gone to medical school,
But instead she wants to be a goddess.

Plastic surgery costs a million.
Legal school isn't THAT much.
Now you even look like plastic,
And feel like it to the touch.

Oh stupid, stupid Barbie,
You've changed so many girls.
They act so prissy and so snobby,
It makes me want to hurl.

So many future teachers,
Lawyers, doctors, vets,
Beauty school is all
The education that they'll get.

C'mon, it's not that important,
The way you act or look.
Beauty products aren't good friends.
Some better ones are books.

by Stephanie Anderson (age 12)

Stephanie Anderson was in sixth grade when she wrote this poem. On the cusp of adolescence, she had the strength of her own convictions and the willingness to state them openly, publishing them for the world to see. Soon, though, psychologists and sociologists warn us, Stephanie's body will change and with it her resolve not to "act so prissy and so snobby." Stephanie, too, may begin to worry more about looks than books, more about popularity than personhood.

Though girls begin this first change of life at increasingly younger ages, it is in middle or junior high school that their new personalities more clearly emerge. Several years ago, I did an ethnographic study of literacy in the eighth grade. It had been my intention to see what "eighth grade" and "eighth graders" might look like in different schools and in different cultural settings, and what "literacy" might mean in each. Thus, I became a participant-observer in Priscilla's class at Bennett, a public middle school in a small but rapidly growing suburban town, and in Betsy's class at Our Lady, a private Catholic academy for girls. Each school had something called "the eighth grade." I wondered how similar those eighth grades really were. Though the two schools are in the Philadelphia metropolitan area, within thirty minutes' drive of each other, they often seemed worlds apart as I drove from one to the other almost daily from January through June.

As part of the study, I taught a writing unit in each classroom. The assignment was the same: Create a character, any character of interest to you, and follow that character into his or her story. Each class did the same character-creating activities the same way: The teacher and I modeled together, the students followed our lead. Then students paired up, introduced their characters to each other, and wrote dialogues to help develop each character's voice. Finally, they moved to the story writing itself. The unit was intended to reveal similarities or differences in students' understanding of narrative writing and fiction across these culturally different settings, which it did. It seems important to share here that the stories also carried powerful messages about how girls understand their place in the world and how they are empowered by the culture in which they live.

Choices and Chances: Stories from Our Lady Academy

Our Lady Academy is a school with a singular cultural message so explicitly delivered as to seem almost simplistic at times. The girls hear the message in all their classes, religious and secular. They hear it in everything from annual Mission Days, to monthly religious services and Respect Life programs, to daily announcements and cafeteria practices. Our Lady girls are doubly blessed, the school and its teachers point out at every opportunity. God loves them and their parents do too. As recipients of this love, these blessings, Our Lady girls have responsibilities to themselves, their parents, their community, and their God. If they live up to these gifts and responsibilities, the blessings will continue. If they fall short, however, the blessings will cease and punishment will ensue instead. So says the school culture, and so say all the stories these girls wrote.

Stories written by girls at Our Lady look perfect. Of the nineteen completed, all but two are typed; many are presented in plastic covers with colorful bindings. The shortest story is three pages long; the longest, nine; the average, between three and four. Despite the unconstrained assignment, all nineteen stories focus on girls or young women living their lives. Some of the protagonists are heroes, some villains, and some victims. Some plots are romantic, some realistic, and some fantastic. Many resemble the after-school specials and other teenager-aimed television dramas and adolescent novels so popular with these girls. Yet none of these stories diverges from the how-to-live-successfully-as-a-woman theme.

Our Lady students' protagonists divide neatly into three variations on this consistent theme: (1) females whose innocence or good deeds are rewarded, sooner or later, with happy lives and the esteem of others; (2) females whose guilt or bad deeds are punished, either by death or a profoundly sadder but wiser future; and (3) females who by dying innocently from illness or accident provide models for others and who, though gone, are never forgotten.

Stories in all three categories share an understanding of where power lies in an individual female's life. All the characters, for good or for ill, ostensibly control their own lives and futures through their own choices and actions. I say "ostensibly" because the criteria determining whether their choices and actions yield success or failure—blessing or punishment—are the "good girl/bad girl" criteria that have permeated American culture since its inception. They are the criteria of an ultimate justice that prefers innocence, honesty, and selflessness in women above all else.

Consider Ambar Ridgeway Young, the 24-year-old FBI homicide detective in "The Dying Cop." (She is one of several professional women in these stories. The others include a veterinarian and a woman who is an algebra teacher by day, an artist by night.) Ambar grew up "in the Beacon Hill section of Boston." As a girl, Ambar watched a murderer slit her father's throat as her father tried to help the attacker's previous victim. Then she saw her mother die "of an instant heartattack [sic] humble person she was." That traumatic experience "gave [Ambar] the determination to help the world become better and enter the police academy . . . [She] decided, when entering the force, never to have a husband or bare [sic] children for [she did] not want to endanger anyone else's life but [her] own."

Ambar has only two important people in her life: a "wonderful" partner, Baxter Colin Craye, and "an elderly lady who was like a mother to me," Lady Tressilian. The plot of the story involves Ambar solving a series of murders committed identically to her father's. The climax comes as Lady Tressilian is about to become the killer's next victim because of her relationship to Ambar. After stopping the attempted murder with "one good shot," Ambar "knelt down and took Lady in [her] arms."

> I felt awfully bad that her life was in danger because of my occupation. I never wanted to get too close to anyone, or have anyone love me because I loved my parents and they died. I went through a great hardship after that accepting that they weren't here anymore. I didn't want anyone to go through that if I died in the line of duty or have anyone miss me. A gentle hand on my shoulder interrupted my thoughts. "Baxter Colin Craye, where have you been?" I looked at him with tears in my eye and gave a great sigh of relief. I felt better that he was here now. I did learn one thing today that there are going to be a few good people who will miss me.

Innocent and altruistic, making all the right choices, Ambar is rewarded.

Then there is Scarlet—typical of the many teenage protagonists in Our Lady girls' stories. "Little Miss Perfect" to her jealous classmates, Scarlet has been physically and sexually abused by her father. Her efforts to conceal this secret form the plot of this five-chapter story, in which Scarlet's best friend Jen pieces together the clues. Titled "The Not So Perfect," the story ends in the girls' locker room at school, with Jen confronting Scarlet and Scarlet dissolving into tears after insisting, "He doesn't mean to hurt me," "I'm just not good enough," "He needs me to love him," and "He needs me ever since mom left." (Not that she blames her mother: "My mom left us when I was seven. She never loved us. She couldn't.") The story concludes: "Scarlet's perfect life no longer seemed so perfect to Jen. It took Scarlet years of therapy to deal with her numerous problems. Jen never left her side through the whole terrible ordeal." Another innocent female who only wants to protect those she loves is ultimately saved and rewarded for being a good girl.

Seven Our Lady girls wrote such virtue-rewarded stories in which innocence, honesty, selflessness, or some combination of these characteristics allows females to attain the rewards they deserve. Eight girls, however, wrote stories in which teenage girls, frequently described as wealthy and spoiled, are punished for being less than good, making less-than-virtuous choices.

In "A Hard Lesson to Learn," Dominique throws a Saturday night party, "not a slumber party—she's way too cool for them," and invites all the "hottest seniors." Her best friend Skie, only a sophomore, gets drunk and is offered cocaine by Chris, the captain of the football team.

> "This stuff is decent, man [Skie says]. Where'd ya get it?"
> "Listen I have a supply of it for you, " Chris said.
> Skie was a rich girl and had plenty of money for it.
> "Alls ya have to do is give me $100 dollars and its yours."
> "Really? Here it is." Skie said ripping out $100 like it was a dollar.

Dominique sees this transaction, tries to take the cocaine from Skie, fails, then insists Skie "get out of [her] house." Feeling scared after Skie has fled, Dominique tries to persuade Chris to go after her, but he refuses. "Chill," he tells her. "She hasn't had it that long."

Suddenly, brakes squeal outside. Skie, drunk on beer and high on cocaine, has been struck and killed by a drunk driver.

> "Oh my god! It's all my fault! I should've never let her go home. She shouldn't of left my sight until I took those drugs away from her. It's all my fault. I'm never going to forgive myself!" Dominique cried.
>
> After many weeks of going to a counselor, Dominique learned a lesson of a lifetime—the hard way. From now on she will be sticking to slumber parties and will never let a friend go alone if they are in trouble.
>
> As for coping with her best friend's death, she will never get over it. Her parents, friends, and family give her all the support she needs. And every night she says a prayer that kids don't ever drink or do drugs under pressure or because they think it's cool.

Skie, who chooses to use alcohol and drugs, dies. Dominique, who creates the context in which Skie makes her choice, then chooses not to stop her, does not die but suffers and lives on, sadder but wiser. Typical of so many Our Lady protagonists involved in substance abuse, lying, stealing, and even a status-climbing murder-suicide, these two girls control their lives and get what their choices deserve in the universe these writers understand.

One story from Our Lady shows just how powerful individual choices seem to these girls, how they affect—or haunt—women for years, even long after they are made. Valerie Hudson, protagonist of this untitled tale, is buying her wedding gown when she hears "horrible sounds outside of the store." She goes outside, runs

> . . . up the alley, and lying there [is] a girl screaming with blood all over the cold concrete. Valerie [takes] a close look and [runs] away with horror building up inside her body. She [gets] home and [goes] to bed with terrifying nightmares: she [is] putting herself in the girl's place. The next morning she [is] sweating nervously at what she had seen the night before in the alley. She decide[s] to tell no one.

The story does not end there, however. Ten years later, Valerie returns to the same shop to purchase her daughter's First Holy Communion dress, "and guess who she bumped into? The girl who she failed to help ten years ago. . . . The girl did notice Valerie and gave her a dirty look saying, 'I am going to get you back'." The nightmares return but Valerie "still doesn't let anyone know the secret that is burning in her heart."

Five additional years pass. The girl—now a famous rock star—appears at Valerie's door, a knife in her hand.

> Valerie runs from room to room trying to lock the doors. Finally she surrenders and is killed in an instant. She was stabbed seven times. Missy Steel, the famous rock star, pleaded her case all the way to the Supreme Court. It is still undecided after fifteen years. This case became known all around the world as Hudson vs. Steel.

Unlike other protagonists in the Our Lady girls' stories, Valerie is punished not for what she does, but for what she fails to do. Despite the good life she leads for fifteen years as church member, wife, and mother, her consciously chosen, twice-committed sins of omission ultimately take her life. Curiously, Valerie's murderer is not condemned immediately and may not be condemned at all. So Valerie learns her lesson the hardest possible way, getting what she deserves, what she chooses for herself. Justice will be served in this Our Lady student's universe, even long after the fact.

The remaining subset of Our Lady stories reconfirms the existence of ideal, ultimate justice in the world. These four stories present women losing battles with cancer, AIDS (contracted through a blood transfusion), and an earthquake, all what some would call acts of God. Each victim chooses to die well, to die bravely, and each leaves behind a best friend or, in one case, a teenage daughter. These survivors "will never forget" those who die; they will go on to live better lives in memory of the gone-but-not-forgotten one who chose to live—and die—as a woman should.

It is difficult to credit coincidence for the consistent moral-seeking nature of these stories from Our Lady. It is equally difficult to credit coincidence for the shared definitions of good and bad. That these girls use stories to teach overt moral lessons, that they believe in ultimate justice, that they see women in control of their lives only to the extent to which they make the right choices according to a shared set of moral precepts, is testimony to the effectiveness of the all-pervasive culture of their school. No one who spends time in Our Lady Academy could deny the clear correlation between the culture of the school and the perceptions of these girls about what it means to be a woman.

Winning and Losing at Bennett Middle School

What about the girls at Bennett? What do their stories reveal about the power that they believe women have over their own lives? Without consistent, overt moral strictures imposed by their school, do they imagine women in total control, without threat of punishment or chastisement of any sort? That is, in fact, what Bennett boys' stories suggest about males, that they have total control of their lives, but those are stories for another article. Bennett girls' stories reveal a different perspective entirely.

Ten girls wrote stories at Bennett, seven about females apart from male-female relationships, three about "girlfriends" (a category notably unimportant at Our Lady). Among the seven autonomous female protagonists are an undercover police officer, a twenty-first-century scientist, a prize-winning equestrienne, a drummer in a rock band, and three teenage or younger girls still in school. Of these seven females, not one succeeds in reaching her goals, regardless of what those goals are. These females fail not because they are "bad" by any particular universal standard of good and evil. Rather, they fail for minor infractions or oversights, or for no discernable reasons at all. In fact, Bennett girls' stories suggest that neither justice nor rationale exist in their worlds; things just happen to women. Female protagonists in these stories either lose (read: are punished) or fear losing (read: fear punishment), and they rarely get a second chance, no matter how much sadder-but-wiser they are.

In "Fast Times at Barnnett High," Allison Lee, "undercover cop," is on the verge of breaking up a drug-dealing ring after months of work posing as a student at the school. She has almost all the evidence she needs to convict the captain of the football team; all that remains is to catch him with his supplier. Allison waits in the locker room for the final showdown.

> Suddenly I heard Kurt's loud obnoxious voice. I ducked behind a dumpster. Luckily, I had my gun. I quickly made my move. I jumped out. "FREEZE, POLICE. PUT YOUR HANDS IN THE AIR NOW!" I was about to read them their rights when a shot rang out and I felt searing pain shoot through my spine. Then everything went dark.

That shot puts Allison in a wheelchair for life. The story ends:

> It's been five years now since the shooting . . . I think maybe I should have waited and called some back-up. I've somewhat adjusted to this awful life even though I can't do what I love, which is fighting crime. Carlos Lopez ["the boss"] is awaiting trial even to this day for illegal drugs, selling, buying, trafficking, and of course, attempted murder. I live for the day that that evil man is put behind bars where he belongs. He is the one person who has shown me that life in a wheelchair is the hardest thing I'll ever have to face.

Brave, caring, one of the "good guys," Allison is punished while the man who destroys the life she loves may never be tried or convicted. Is it only "luck" that she had her gun with her, as this writer suggests? Is she punished for overreaching, for not calling "some back-up," trying to succeed alone? If she were Allan instead of Allison, would such seemingly heroic behavior condemn her to a wheelchair for life? Or is there simply no justice in the world?

The ways of Bennett girls' perceived world do not change much in the twenty-first century, not even for Sara, a character who "believed in democracy, and freedom, and equal rights for all people," and whose boyfriend, Ian, fought and died in World War III. After Ian's death, Sara, who was "a college zoology major," earns her doctorate to become "one of the world's most important ecological scientists, doing groundbreaking research almost as a daily routine." When offered the chance to work on Mars, at "the perfect human-made Earth-like environment . . . to introduce various endangered species into the especially successful biomes," Sara accepts and moves to Space Station Demeter.

One night Sara's sister, who narrates this story, receives a phone call. Sara is dead, killed in an attack on Mars' military base, Valkyrie. What was Sara doing at Valkyrie? Why wasn't she at Demeter?

> It is a complete mystery why she went there . . . The people at Demeter say she left a note saying she was going to Valkyrie but gave no reason why. It remains a mystery. And a tragedy.

The writer offers no suggestion of reason or justice in this story, no hint of overreaching, oversight, or other flaw on Sara's part. There is simply no justice in the world, no control over one's life — only mystery and tragedy.

In addition to actual tragedy, there is also fear of tragedy in Bennett girls' stories. Two revolve around fearful dreams, a third around a fearful secret that must be kept. "Dream or Reality?" is the story of Chelsea McGovern's dream about receiving a long-awaited phone call announcing that her band (interestingly named "Out of Control") will have a recording tryout with a major record company. Terrifically excited, Chelsea calls the other band members, dresses with care, and leaves for the studio, only to forget her drumsticks. She returns home, grabs the sticks, and zooms off again, this time stopping for food at a drive-through because she now has no time to eat otherwise. Driving away from the restaurant, she inadvertently "ran a red light and headed straight for a car coming in the opposite direction."

Just as Chelsea screams at the impending crash, her roommate enters and wakes her up because "The phone is for you . . . Some guy. I think he said he was calling about your band, 'Out of Control'."

> "OH NO!" [Chelsea screams.]
> "What's wrong? Shouldn't that be good?" [Her roommate asks.]
> "Well it would be good if I hadn't gone to sleep last night."

Feel free to dream, this story suggests, but be sure to dream of all the possibilities. Is Chelsea overreaching? Is it inappropriate for a girl to dream of becoming a drummer in a rock band? Are the carelessness of forgetting drumsticks and the irresponsibility of being late and running a red light evidence of character sufficiently flawed to deserve death? I doubt that I would ask these questions of Chelsea's story had I not read it in the context of Bennett Middle School juxtaposed with Our Lady Academy.

In fact, I might not have asked those questions if I had not read another Bennett girl's story, about a young girl named Bobby Joe, who is "a tomboy" and "outspoken" and "nicknamed Tadpole because of her love to fish." Bobby Joe, who one night dreams about reeling in the locket her mother always wore and "knowing" it means her mother and father are dead, drowned in the creek near the house. Bobby Joe, who, after that dream, "swore right then and there that she would never again eat a whole half gallon of chocolate, rocky-road, marshmallow, peanut butter ice cream with chocolate syrup, cherries, and extra nuts right before she goes to bed!"

And, I probably would not have asked those questions had I not read another Bennett girl's story, about Victoria McDevitt, "daddy's perfect little girl," daughter of a wealthy family. Victoria earns straight As in school, studies French, and "knows that she would receive a special gift for her accomplishments" as a prize-winning rider of show horses—only if daddy never learns "Victoria's Secret," that eight-year-old Victoria still "wet [her] panties."

Being forgetful and late, overeating, and incontinence certainly are not the major crimes (or sins) with which Our Lady girls' stories are concerned. Nor are they the sorts of problems that males encounter in stories written by the Bennett boys. Fear of failure, "pigging out," and wetting one's pants seem painfully female concerns—female flaws—which have potentially painful, if not lethal, results in Bennett girls' minds.

The three remaining stories by these girls are "girlfriend" stories. In all three the female protagonists have happy endings. One of them, "blond haired, blue eyed, attractive" Sue, with the "soft, happy, peaceful voice," wins

David, who "got nervous around girls" and generally preferred his music (he's a saxophone player) and his "red corvette" to their company. But Sue is a musician, too, and "like[s] the same mystery books and the same foods" as David. So he "knew this was going to last some time," and Sue is glad.

Trixia helps "poor betrayed Herbert" recover from Bev, the girlfriend who made his life wonderful "until [she] was accepted into [the popular] group and dropped Herbert for good." And Sara is faithful sidekick to her friend Chris Mambazio, traveling to Africa with him to help him find his birth parents.

Girls who are pretty, good, and helpful get or keep their men. And keeping a man is the only way girls win at Bennett.

How is Bennett Middle School delivering these seemingly clear messages to its students? Unlike the overtly stated message at Our Lady Academy, the one absorbed by students in this public school is much less consistent or explicit. While the "BMS Student Handbook" encourages students—or warns them—to "show respect" to everyone, to "be aware of all rules and regulations" and follow them, to "strive to do [their] best," and to "become more responsible for [their] personal growth and academic success," little else is done on a regular or schoolwide basis besides the occasional antidrug assembly program.

Perhaps because Bennett teachers, administrators, and parents represent a wide range of beliefs, multiple messages can coexist in this school culture. Perhaps because most of these messages go unarticulated most of the time, however, students must discern the messages for themselves. What each student understands in terms of values, beliefs, and expectations, therefore, is mediated through peers and delivery systems other than the school itself. As a result, the dominant messages of popular and traditional middle-class American culture seem to permeate Bennett more by osmosis and omission than intention. However unintentional the messages may be, however, Bennett students' stories indicate that these suggestions are clearly heard.

Other Answers, Other Questions

While this account is primarily about girls' perceptions of female power, their sense of the control women have over their own lives, it seems important to at least briefly note their male classmates' perceptions on this point. For as I have suggested, girls' perceptions are not created in a vacuum; they are at least partially produced by the cultural context in which they are created, and male perceptions are part of that cultural milieu.

How do adolescent boys view female empowerment in these settings? From Our Lady, there are, of course, no male stories to report. At Bennett, what might be expected from a mainstream public school is exactly what emerges in the boys' writing. Female characters are not just actual or potential losers in girls' stories. They lose in boys' stories as well, with only three exceptions among the fifteen stories written by boys. In these, three pretty, good, smart, sweet, or sexy girls "win": The heroes love them. Males, on the other hand, consistently win, according to Bennett boys. Whether athlete or drug dealer, adult or adolescent, good or evil by traditional standards, Bennett boys see males controlling what happens in their lives. Males have the power that females lack.

This is not to suggest that all male protagonists created by Bennett boys succeed. In fact, there are three stories among the fifteen in which traditional Judeo-Christian morality prevails and evildoers are punished, but those few only highlight the fact that these mainstream, white, adolescent males believe that the power in their lives is theirs. "Be all that you can be" has unambiguous meaning for white males, these boys suggest. It is much more complicated—and conflicting—for girls of any color.

The awareness that females fear failure, consider relationships primary, or are overly concerned with being pretty and being good is not news. Researchers such as Matina Hoerner and Carol Gilligan have been telling us that for years, and teacher-researchers such as Maureen Barbieri have more recently confirmed those findings. But girls' perceptions of how the universe operates in terms of females, their notions of right, wrong, and justice have not often been addressed. Add to that the apparent relationship between these perceptions and school culture, and these stories by eighth-grade girls in southeastern Pennsylvania take on new meaning and foreground new questions. What messages do schools and their attendant communities send about what women can expect in their lives? What accounts for the sense of impending failure at Bennett? Which would we prefer: the double-edged vision of Our Lady, in which females control their lives as long as they are "good," or the powerlessness and looming fate of Bennett females? And what can we do to keep these from being our only choices and the only choices of the girls in our classrooms?

There are no easy answers to these questions, no quick solutions to the problems they represent. What we as teachers can do in our classrooms, however, is make these questions explicit in ways that let students themselves think about them. Regardless of setting—public, private, or parochial; urban, suburban, or rural; middle school, junior high, or high school—we can help our students explore and question the choices available in the worlds around them, including those presented by our curricula. Just as we want students to question the gender roles portrayed on after-school specials and "Melrose Place," on Oprah and Montel, so we should teach girls – and boys—to question the gender roles presented in even the canonical, seemingly safe literature in the anthologies and trade books we assign.

In the short stories of a popular "silver" literature anthology intended for eighth graders, all of the female protanonists but one are surrounded by smarter, more active men and boys. Clear messages are sent by these characters, who include a modern damsel in distress (Doyle), a beloved wife (Buck), a bemused mother (Jackson), an intimidated governess (Chekov), and a "large woman with a large purse that had everything in it but hammer and nails" (Hughes). In that same anthology, most of the other stories portray no significant female characters at all.

I'm not suggesting that we not teach these stories; I am suggesting that we teach them differently. If we raise questions about these women—and the men in their lives—we model the sort of resistant reading we want our students to do as they read their worlds that surround and produce these words.

On some level, our girls know that it's not only men and boys who are heroes. They know from their own painful experience that not only men and boys "come of age." We should encourage them to notice that *The Tragedy of Othello* is not his alone, nor is Hamlet's. Perhaps if girls are encouraged to ask, "What about Desdemona's tragedy? Ophelia's? Gertrude's?" they will remember that they, too, once knew how to write a poem like "Plastic Princess."

PART II

Transforming Curriculum

The vast majority of women who have moved through the decades have done so without the recognition they so richly deserve. And yet, without their contributions to American life and culture, each generation building on the foundations laid by the previous generation— standing on their mothers' shoulders—the history of America would be unrecognizable to our eyes.
        —CHRISTINE LUNARDINI, *"Introduction,"*
    What Every Woman Should Know About Women's History

3

Reaching and Teaching Girls

Gender and Literacy Across the Middle School Curriculum

JANET J. MONTELARO

Over the past thirty years, women's studies has produced volumes of knowledge about gender in virtually every academic discipline in higher education. Research about girls and women in the fields of medicine, biology, psychology, education, history, science, mathematics, language, literature, communication, music, religion, health science, and sports has provided educators with new material to consider in revising and updating curricula and teaching methods. Pedagogy in grades six through twelve must also reflect this new information about gender if basic education is to realize its potential for benefiting all students. The extent to which we incorporate this new scholarship will determine the extent to which we raise our students' and our own awareness about gender issues and will determine the level of "gender literacy" in our schools.

In this chapter, I highlight some of the research on girls and classroom climates that has emerged in the past decade, which provides the rationale for change. Then I suggest specific ways to integrate gender-balanced content and feminist pedagogy into the middle school curriculum, specifically into social studies, health, science, mathematics, computer science, and language arts courses.

A Decade of Research on Girls

Increasingly, research about gender is bringing to the attention of educators and parents the particular kinds of risks that schoolgirls face. In 1991, the American Association of University Women (AAUW) published a groundbreaking study, *Shortchanging Girls, Shortchanging America,* which found that

23

as girls approach adolescence, they undergo a more severe decline in self-esteem than do adolescent boys. This study caught the attention of the media nationwide and underscored the relevance of other research showing that girls are systematically, if unintentionally, discouraged from a wide range of academic pursuits, particularly in math and science. A more extensive report, *How Schools Shortchange Girls* (AAUW 1992), documented the many ways in which American public schools benefit boys more than girls, resulting in a dramatic gender gap in most academic subjects. Just as startling are the findings that school curricula either stereotype or ignore girls and women altogether, that sexual harassment of girls is an increasingly serious problem, and that standardized test scores continue to show a gender gap that has a debilitating effect on girls' career choices.

Peggy Orenstein's influential book, *School Girls: Young Women, Self Esteem, and the Confidence Gap* (1994), which follows the activities of middle school girls in two California public schools, points to the complexity of their behaviors and beliefs. Orenstein noted perfectionism, defeatism, lack of confidence, and a deflated sense of self-worth that often predict varying degrees of academic failure for girls. During that same year, clinical psychologist Mary Pipher published case studies of adolescent girls in her best-seller *Reviving Ophelia: Saving the Selves of Adolescent Girls.* Pipher looked closely at the multidimensional aspects of girls' development—physical, social, cognitive, academic, spiritual, emotional, and psychological—and at how girls confront the numerous challenges common to many adolescents, including eating disorders, peer and family relationships, drugs and alcohol, depression, sex, violence, and teen pregnancy. Pipher reminds us how difficult it is for girls to develop healthy identities in a culture that is often hostile to and ignores their development and their achievements. She compares adolescence to a hurricane that many girls eventually weather with their sense of self intact. For others who are emotionally and psychologically more fragile, a nurturing and conscientious effort must be made on the part of teachers, counselors, and parents if girls are to succeed in facing the challenges of becoming adult women.

Myra and David Sadker, prominent researchers in gender and education, demonstrate through meticulous observation that gender bias exists from the primary grades through higher education; more importantly, bias among teaching professionals, both in the curriculum and in the ways that material is taught, is largely unconscious and unintentional (*Failing at Fairness,* 1994). Consciousness about gender issues doesn't only mean addressing stereotypes that denigrate girls and women. It also means raising consciousness about how we teach in a mixed-sex environment; deciding what information we choose to teach and how we prioritize the information we choose to impart;

and understanding how we allow and encourage male and female students to interact in the learning environment. It means becoming more aware of those pedagogical behaviors that the Sadkers term "micro-inequities" (2), those small, unconscious decisions and activities in our teaching that accumulate to produce a disadvantaged academic playing field for female students.

More recently, the AAUW published *Girls in the Middle: Working to Succeed in School* (Cohen and Blanc 1996), which identifies concrete strategies that middle school girls use to deal effectively with social and academic challenges. The study identifies three coping techniques or roles that girls adopt to help them gain confidence and bolster their newly emerging identities as adolescents. The first is "speaking out," whereby girls are assertive and make themselves heard. The second is "doing school," where girls work hard academically to meet the demands of their teachers in commendable ways. The third is "crossing borders," where girls demonstrate the ability to move within and fit into different groups based on ethnicity, class, or race, or even between the world of adults and peer groups. This study is significant because it documents some of the ways girls succeed in the middle school environment, but it also points out how we often misinterpret girls' coping behaviors. The report includes recommendations on how to support middle school girls and enhance their emotional and academic development.

Individual Differences and Classroom Climate

A hasty decision educators often make when considering the topic of gender equity in the classroom is to pay more attention to female students, simply giving them more opportunities to participate in the learning process and to have their points of view heard. While these actions are laudable, they offer only a partial remedy. Women's and gender studies research in education has taught us that our classrooms can be places of hostility for those who are at a disadvantage in the school population because of gender, sexual orientation, race, social class, ethnic background, special abilities or disabilities, or any combination of these factors. When students feel relegated to the margins, the classroom becomes a threatening environment for them and learning ceases. Typically, the term "disadvantaged" simply means "different." Difference may refer to any category in which a student is in the minority with regard to what is being taught and to whom it is being taught, as well as under what conscious or unconscious assumptions the teacher is imparting knowledge. Difference in the classroom, then, can be based not only on gender, but also on ethnicity, nationality, race, economic class, disability, age, sexual orientation, or any other category that can be used to distinguish one student from another.

In the early 1980s, Roberta M. Hall and Bernice R. Sandler found women's experiences in college and university learning environments to be different from men's. They used the term "chilly climate" to describe the negative influence on women students that is produced by the many small inequities that, taken together, create a chilling environment. In light of their work, some institutions noted how faculty members and their teaching styles inadvertently produce a negative learning atmosphere for women. Fourteen years later, Sandler and Hall, along with Lisa Silverberg, authored *The Chilly Classroom Climate: A Guide to Improve the Education of Women* (1996). Their more comprehensive Chilly Climate study detailed the many ways women are treated differently in the classroom. It identifies how women and men tend to use speech and language differently and notes how both gender and race affect speech and language use in the learning environment. It suggested teaching strategies that work best for women, and offered new methods for teachers and administrators to increase women's participation and positive learning experiences in the classroom. The Chilly Climate study has led to the appearance of books designed for use in elementary and secondary schools. For example, Dianne D. Horgan's teacher workbook *Achieving Gender Equity* (1995) is designed especially for K–12 teachers who want to assess the degree of gender equity in their classrooms and to learn new strategies for teaching with less gender bias.

Sexual harassment is one of the most pervasive problems negatively affecting self-esteem and academic success in today's schools. *Hostile Hallways,* the first national study of the extent of sexual harassment in U.S. public schools, was commissioned by the AAUW in 1993. Researchers found that a staggering 85 percent of sexual harassment victims are girls, and that 76 percent of all boys claim to have been victims of sexual harassment. Though the percentage of boys who are harassed is also high, the study found that girls experience a more enduring negative impact from sexual harassment in terms of their self-esteem and self-confidence in their academic work. Just as girls are affected more than boys are, African American girls feel the impact more deeply than do girls of other races. The study also reported that homophobia—fearful and prejudicial attitudes about gays and lesbians, which lead to verbal abuse and often violence—starts as early in the educational system as elementary school.

Any form of sexual harassment, including homophobic abuse, is debilitating not only to the students who are direct victims, but to the entire student body as well. Throughout the school, because students live in fear of becoming the next victim, they help keep each other in place either through their actions or through their silent complicity. It is important to notice that behaviors, speech patterns, clothing styles, and gestures that are considered "feminine" are often the basis of comments constituting sexual harassment.

Middle school girls lament that the very term "girl" connotes weakness and inferiority when spoken in a condescending, accusatory, or hostile manner. Boys often fear correction by their male peers for walking, running, throwing, or otherwise acting in a manner considered to be "like a girl," whatever the activity under scrutiny.

Homophobic slurs are often used to keep boys and girls within a strict dichotomy of masculine and feminine gender roles, for fear of being labeled gay or lesbian. Public schools are often bastions of sexual harassment and homophobia, where students participate in verbal violence about gender and expect, in many cases, to get away with it. Alarming anecdotal evidence from many of my students who are training to become teachers suggests that their own high school and middle school teachers engaged in this name-calling and stereotyping. They report that many of their teachers made hostile comments about women, girls, lesbians, and gays, or often pretended not to hear when students did so. Barbara Smith (1998, 113) constructs the following rationale for homophobic sexual harassment:

> There are numerous reasons for otherwise sensitive people's reluctance to confront homophobia in themselves and others. A major one is that people are generally threatened about issues of sexuality, and for some the mere existence of homosexuals calls their sexuality/heterosexuality into question. Unlike many oppressed groups, homosexuals are not a group whose identity is clear from birth. Through the process of coming out, a person might indeed acquire this identity at any point in life. One way to protect one's heterosexual credentials and privilege is to put down lesbians and gay men at every turn, to make as large a gulf as possible between "we" and "they."

Schools with the best policies on sexual harassment can suffer from a chilly atmosphere if teachers do not actively enforce the guidelines. Teachers can reduce the threat that produces such hostility in their schools and classrooms by insisting on respect, tolerance, and civil discourse for all students. Materials are now available for teachers who wish to educate students to become more tolerant. An excellent textbook, *Dealing with Differences: Taking Action on Class, Race, Gender and Disability* (Ellis and Llewellyn 1997, 79–102), has a special section that introduces students to gender differences, sexism, and heterosexism.

Speaking frankly with middle school students about differences in sexual orientation helps students shed many of the false assumptions and fears they may have about lesbian and gay sexual identity. One in ten individuals in our society is gay or lesbian. Anguish about sexual identity is one of the major causes of depression and suicide among adolescents. Sexual harassment is a human rights issue because it is a form of prejudice that can lead to social ostracism, job discrimination, and violence. Schools must revise or adopt conduct policies on sexual harassment; teachers must make it a priority to understand the subtleties of this form of abuse and educate students to be more sensitive toward and tolerant of others.

Revising the Curriculum to Account for Gender

Social Studies and History

In a suburban Pittsburgh school district where I have served as a consultant for secondary curriculum revision, I was asked to evaluate the content of social studies courses with regard to their pertinence to women and girls. I asked teachers who were responsible for revising the curriculum several questions. I asked sixth grade world geography teachers to consider how women are represented, if at all, in their geography materials and whether global and international representations of the kinds of work women do, both inside and outside of the home, were sufficiently varied. In developing countries, women's prominent roles in agriculture and food production, as well as their contributions to cultural life, should be taken into account. I also asked the teachers to locate examples that contradict stereotypical representations of women as consumers and men as producers, since both men and women are usually responsible for both of these realms in any regional economy. I suggested that students could be asked to research how the distribution of global resources affects the social realities of women and children in developing countries or how women's social and economic conditions differ between Western and Eastern countries. Teachers might guide student research through a library search or online information sources such as the Smithsonian Institution, the National Geographic Society, and newspapers with international perspectives such as the *New York Times*.

The seventh-grade social studies curriculum focuses on Western civilization, beginning with prehistorical times and introducing students to the ancient civilizations of the Middle East. First, I asked teachers to consider women's roles in prehistorical communities before the emergence of patriarchy. This question still surprises many teachers who have never been introduced to Gerda Lerner's important study *The Creation of Patriarchy* (1986), which argues that men's subordination of women was not biologically determined but was, rather, a historical process that emerged gradually over twenty-five hundred years. Similarly, Lerner's *The Creation of Feminist Consciousness* (1993) follows women's systematic exclusion from formal education and traces women's contributions to the history of thought from the Middle Ages through the nineteenth century.

My son's seventh-grade social studies textbook was a "revised" edition that claimed greater diversity and inclusion as one of its advantages. I discovered that the editors of this edition simply kept the original text, but inserted pages about historical women and Eastern cultures as "enrichment" sections. While this "revision" was certainly preferable to the former text, which was completely Eurocentric and focused on wars and famous male rulers, scholars such as Charlotte Bunch (1987, 140) remind us that inclusion of women's and gender issues is not simply a formula whereby we "add women and stir." A transformation model for inclusion, which seeks to question underlying assumptions about Western culture, produces a very different picture of Western civilization once women's contributions are acknowledged and placed in their proper contexts.

The seventh-grade social studies course also presents early formations of democratic states but ignores women's historic, systematic exclusion from the privileges of democracy. Feminist theorists note that democracies continue to fail to confer equal privileges on women. Teachers who have their students examine Plato's and Aristotle's views on the social status of women will create a unique opportunity to reflect with students on some classical roots of misogynist thinking that are pervasive today.

In addition, I asked teachers to consider these questions: What was the extent of women's education in the classical societies of Greece and Rome? Who are the significant women that participated in the early schools of mathematics and philosophy? Slowly, this information is filtering down to teachers and textbooks, but unless teachers make an effort to update their curricula, students will not have any awareness of women's roles in and contributions to Western history. This information gap shortchanges boys and girls.

The eighth-grade American history course covers the periods of colonization, the American Revolution, westward expansion, the Civil War, and Reconstruction. Because the syllabus called for examining the roles and contributions of people from a variety of cultures, such as Native Americans and African Americans, and for looking at the influences of a variety of immigrant groups on major historical events and developments, I asked teachers to consider what might be meant by the term "multicultural." Too often, American history in our public schools is presented within a framework that unintentionally considers all nonwhites as the multicultural population in society, and overlooks the fact that "whiteness" represents neither a cohesive nor a monolithic racial group. When students investigate this issue, they find that many members of the group often labeled "white" are the descendants of different groups of Europeans that were themselves subject to various degrees of social ostracism and discrimination, according to their ethnicity and the historical period of their emigration. I asked teachers to add other groups that were not included in the present syllabus, such as Jewish Americans, Hispanic Americans, and Asian Americans, all of which are quite varied in their language, ethnicity, and cultural and religious heritage. I also encouraged strategies for presenting the multitude of Native American cultures so that they would not appear homogenous or vaguely generalized. One way to do this is to develop a more detailed picture of the social and political centrality of women in specific Native American cultures.

In the American colonial era, women's social realities extended beyond the domestic sphere. Many affordable reference books on women's history are now available and should be purchased by schools for classroom and library use. For example, Lunardini's *What Every American Should Know About Women's History* (1997) supplies abundant examples of women's social and political activities since the earliest settlements in America. Women had active roles in land ownership and management; fought and traveled with armies in both the American Revolution and the Civil War; and participated in and instigated social reform for the abolition of slavery, women's suffrage, temperance, and education. Women were writers, teachers, farmers, mill workers, explorers, inventors, doctors and nurses, theologians, and preachers. Our American history texts usually fail to represent women in this wide variety of activities. The *Women's History Catalog* (National Women's History Project 1999) is an excellent source of books and teaching aids to supplement and enrich the teaching of American history. Parents are often willing to donate these books to the classroom if given the opportunity. With improved resources, students can be assigned interesting research projects that can add new knowledge to their awareness of American history.

By eighth grade, students should have had the opportunity to answer the following questions in some detail: When and how did women begin to challenge social attitudes that barred them from political participation? How did the institution of slavery affect African American men and women differently? What was the relationship between the abolition movement and the women's suffrage movement? What famous American women helped the cause of abolition? Who were central figures in the women's suffrage movement? What effect did the Civil War have on the campaign for women's rights? What different roles did women from the North and South serve during the Civil War? How did Constitutional amendments after the Civil War fail to address women's political status? What idea did the Fifteenth Amendment express regarding the relationship between women's citizenship and suffrage?

During Women's History Month, many college students on my campus were asked by a student newspaper reporter to name at least five famous women in American history. Many could not name three. Students should learn about women's history and women's political participation long before they attend college. Political scientists today are assessing how significant gender can be in local and national political elections, and states are now compiling data on women's political participation as voters and as elected officials. This new data increases the relevance of studying women's roles in American history.

Health Education

Health education in middle schools can certainly benefit from women's studies approaches. When I served on a committee to review one school's health services education curriculum, I heard strong negative reactions from some parents. They did not feel that their middle school sons or daughters needed more detailed information on human reproduction, the hormonal and somatic changes boys and girls experience during puberty, and the different behaviors responsible for the contraction of sexually transmitted diseases (STDs) and AIDS. More surprisingly, many certified middle school teachers felt uncomfortable about teaching health issues, even in the context of a science class. Better diets for children and the control of more childhood diseases have caused girls to begin to menstruate earlier; today, the average age is twelve. Many girls experience menarche as early as third grade, and many school health personnel are beginning education about menstruation in the lower elementary grades, even though there is strong resistance to this teaching by some parents. Joan Brumberg (1997, 197) states that today "girls are in trouble because we are experiencing a mismatch between biology and culture" in that girls' early development occurs "within a society that does not protect or nurture them in ways that were once a hallmark of American life."

Our committee recommended that male and female middle school students attend the lectures and film presentations about boys' and girls' puberty and human reproduction together, despite the hostility expressed by some parents. Our rationale was that students in a mixed-sex group would feel a bit more inhibited about making jokes or crude remarks than they would be in single-sex groups. Students had a general question-and-answer session following the presentations. Later they divided into smaller same-sex groups with teachers to discuss questions they might have felt embarrassed to ask in the larger, mixed-sex group. It is the responsibility of teachers to demystify sexual reproduction and bodily functions so students can have more facts to inform the decisions they make about their bodies as they grow older.

Along with other committee members, I examined existing health education materials for gender bias in verbal and visual representations about bodily functions. We also previewed existing films and selected updated teacher aids to replace those that lacked clear information or were too euphemistic. In one film on AIDS, for example, no mention was made that girls are more susceptible than boys to contracting STDs, including AIDS, a fact the news media are only beginning to report. Brumberg recommends that adults increase our advocacy of girls in ways that let us both educate girls about their bodies and nurture their self-esteem.

Many public schools still do not allow the topics of abortion and contraception to be mentioned in school settings, but at the same time, high school girls who will experience consensual sex, rape, and unwanted pregnancy have little or no understanding of their options or rights in these difficult situations. Very few middle schools offer courses on self-esteem, an addition to the health curriculum that seems crucial in light of recent research on girls. Self-esteem courses teach girls about size acceptance and reasonable ranges of weight gain, about how to recognize different kinds of eating disorders and their threat to mental and physical health, about physical and hormonal changes that girls experience, and about different ways to discover and value their uniqueness.

Science, Mathematics, and Computing

In her book *Women in Mathematics: The Addition of Difference,* Claudia Henrion refutes many gender stereotypes that remain prominent in the field of mathematics. Two of her points are especially worth considering if we want to create a better learning environment for middle school girls in math and science. First, she dispels mistaken notions that mathematics is a solitary pursuit and that doing mathematics implies only individual effort. Henrion says, "mathematics is in many ways a highly social activity" but one where "this social dimension often remains invisible" (1997, xxi). Second, Henrion points to prevailing stereotypes that only white males fulfill the predominant images of mathematicians, making it difficult for students to imagine women mathematicians as role models. Despite the fact that many of us have had energetic, brilliant, and highly effective female math teachers, the notion of mathematics as a masculine pursuit remains persistent.

These same assumptions and stereotypes also apply to the world of science. Although women have reached approximately equal levels of representation in the biological sciences and medicine, we are still noticeably underrepresented in the fields of chemistry, physics, and mathematics, and in even more staggering numbers in computer science, engineering, and architecture—fields of study requiring rigorous foundations in science and math. Henrion contends that the problem of imagining women mathematicians (and presumably scientists as well) is more than simply a lack of role models. She examines the tensions between the expectations of the role of mathematician and the stereotypical roles of women (specifically as mothers and romantic partners), which lead some to conclude that women are unsuited for math. Henrion also points to the fact that, throughout history, men have barred women from mathematical education and excluded them from the elite professional societies that encourage and support mathematical research and teaching.

In her book *Reflections on Gender and Science,* Evelyn Fox Keller states that "the identification between scientific thought and masculinity is so deeply embedded in the culture at large that children have little difficulty internalizing it" (1985, 77). Teachers can do much to correct these stereotypes by changing the ways in which students work at mathematical problem solving and scientific investigation. Feminist pedagogy has long encouraged small collaborative groups as a productive way for students to learn, and teachers must take care that girls actually get to do the hands-on work and primary research that the assignments require, not just the more passive tasks of recording and presenting data. Although there is much to be said for same-sex learning in particular situations, both single-sex and mixed-sex groups can work well collaboratively. True collegiality is a valuable skill to teach in the middle grades, and this skill involves sharing the investigative work, the generation of data, the recording and analysis of data, and the writing of lab reports and research papers. Frequent changes in the composition of collaborative groups offers students more opportunities to know one another and to participate in the activities of experimentation, data gathering, and analysis. Students should become conscious in their collaborative work about who is doing the actual science and who is doing the recording, and whether these roles are being shared.

Science and math class should not only be about doing math and science. Students need to do research on the contributions of specific scientists and mathematicians, including women. Who were women's mentors in math and science? Which contemporary women do we know whose professions involve math and science? Which local women professionals could be invited to class to talk about their use of math and science in their work? Reports and interviews about women in science and math should be displayed around the classroom and in the school library. Sue Rosser's *Re-Engineering Female-Friendly Science* (1997) details a step-by-step process for transforming the teaching of science to be more inclusive of women's contributions; to recognize traditional male biases in science; and to maximize girls' participation and interest in science by carefully creating collaborative groups, study groups, and mentoring relationships.

Girls are rapidly closing the gender gap in math and science scores, and educators should take credit for responding appropriately when the alarm was first sounded about this issue. But this gain does not mean that we should ease our efforts to keep girls at high levels of performance in science and math. Rosser notes that "mathematics often becomes the gate-keeping course that determines whether students will be able to pursue courses in science and engineering" (1997, 88). With students tracked into increasingly difficult math courses at early ages, girls often find their interest in math diminished by the end of middle school if they have not been encouraged to succeed in their early math courses. Mary Anne Campbell and Randall K. Campbell-Wright have proposed guidelines for a feminist algebra. They suggest creating nonsexist and female-affirming math texts by rewriting word problems that have gender and misogynistic stereotypes; by adding word problems that represent inclusive and multicultural examples; by analyzing sex similarities and differences in nonarbitrary contexts; and by including examples that represent women's meaningful experiences (Rosser 1995, 128).

In a six-week enrichment course I designed for girls entering sixth grade, women scientists and medical professionals were invited to demonstrate a few science principles by leading the students through a number of experiments, and mathematicians worked with the students on different math problems that had practical applications. This after-school course, Adventures in Science and Math for Girls, had a large and enthusiastic enrollment, and parent volunteers assisted with hands-on projects requiring supervision. One of the visitors was a veterinarian who brought x rays of domestic animals from her office files. Students had to guess what foreign objects animals had ingested, and what medical intervention the veterinarian chose to perform on each animal. Another visitor, a pediatrician, helped us examine a human patient—a twelve-month-old daughter of a teacher. Students were able to listen to respiratory and digestive functions in the infant with stethoscopes we had purchased with the student's registration fees. The students also learned how to measure and record an infant's body temperature, and how to examine an infant's ears for infection.

A paint chemist from a local manufacturing company explained molecular bonding by having the girls move around the room, locking and unlocking hands. She directed students in experiments to show why commercial baby diapers are absorbent, and how chemical bonding works in the manufacture of paints, Silly Putty, and glue. A biochemist brought slides of bacteria to view under microscopes and explained how bacterial infections and antibiotics work. The goal of this course was to have girls work closely with role models who were actively engaged in science and math as part of their everyday work. Each visitor presented her personal story: how she became interested in her profession, why courses in math and science are important, how she overcame obstacles in her career path, and what she found most help-ful in attaining her goal. Most of these women scientists and professionals re-membered a particular teacher who had encouraged them in school and in their choice of career.

The school library agreed to set up a display of posters and books on women scientists and mathematicians during this six-week period, including materials we ordered from the *Women's History Catalog* (National Women's History Project 1999). We also created a photo display of the participating students as they were working at tasks in our course, and students from the entire student body were able to see the different kinds of science and math projects that the girls found enjoyable and interesting.

There should be no question that girls-only opportunities encourage self-confidence in math and science. Teachers of middle school girls know that female students often prefer learning within the contexts of their social groups. This does not mean that we should move to sex-segregated classrooms for math and science, but that we should find ways to provide girls with their own space and peer support in some formal and informal learning environments.

Recent news reports note that there are gender differences in computer skills. Girls use computers as word processors, while boys are more adept at programming functions and at problem solving with computers. Jo Sanders sees today's computer culture as largely male, since most video games and computer software programs are marketed toward boys' and young men's in-terests in conflict, war, destruction, and sexual fantasy (*Teaching the Majority* Roser 1995, 149). Even educational software can be based on themes of con-flict that tend not to interest girls. Sanders' research also shows that girls find computer use more appealing when they are not the minority in the class-room, when they are given opportunities to work in "friendship groups" at the computer, and when computers can be demonstrated to solve real-life problems (Roser, 157).

English and Language Arts

Over the past three decades, feminist pioneers in language and gender stud-ies, such as Robin Lakoff and Dale Spender, have helped raise consciousness about how sexism in language denigrates women and often fails to account for female experiences. Writers and publishers of school textbooks have grad-ually begun to revise vocabulary and language usage to reflect this research. Teachers, however, must still review textbooks carefully for accurate and non-stereotypical representation of girls' and women's experiences. We still see the use of the generic masculine (*man, mankind, he*) in textbooks to refer to all human beings and members of society. Often teachers inadvertently use the generic masculine when creating their own teaching materials for students, and students themselves unconsciously employ these terms when they write.

When I helped edit essays on ecology in a seventh-grade English class, I noted that nearly two-thirds of the class named "man" as a threat to certain endangered species. I briefly explained to students that the use of the generic masculine is confusing, since readers have to determine from the context of the writing whether all human beings are denoted or whether only males are being referred to. Spender (1980, 157) points out that the use of "he" or "man" renders men visible and women invisible. It follows that girls have a more difficult and time-consuming task when reading language that uses the generic masculine, since they have to continually reread for contextual clues as to whether or not they are included in the reference, whereas boys readily assume they are included. Another sexist constraint of language is the use of nonparallel terms whereby the feminine counterparts of masculine terms connote a derogatory or trivial meaning, which tends to mute women and ignore their experiences; for example "a master of his craft," as opposed to a "mistress." In some cases parallel terms do not exist at all. There is no term, for example, to describe women who are sexually healthy, but we do have terms such as "virile" and "potent" to describe such men (Spender 1980, 175).

One way that language arts teachers can actively confront sexism in language is to have students examine stories from mythology and folklore. Traditional fairy tales are being rewritten from women's points of view and with traditional gender roles subverted. Emma Donoghue's *Kissing the Witch* (1997) transforms such tales as "Snow White" and "Beauty and the Beast" with wonderful dramatic effect. When sixth-grade students in a local school recently chose roles from classical mythology and wrote dramatic speeches for their gods and goddesses, many girls chose male roles, since the female roles included only betrayed wives and lovers, nagging wives, and victims of abduction and rape. Here, teachers might have encouraged girls to rewrite the traditional scripts of these "heroines," giving the female characters stronger voices, more personal autonomy, and a greater degree of control over their destinies.

Examples from popular culture offer another alternative for male and female students to study how gender roles are represented in the media, such as magazine advertisements, movies, television programs and commercials, and song lyrics. Stereotypes in media are abundant. Students can easily identify examples in which women and girls are portrayed as weak, dependent, unintelligent, vain, and narcissistic or self-absorbed. Students can further analyze why they think these stereotypes are perpetrated in advertising or television programming, and why they think commercial sponsors would want this type of program or advertisement to represent their products.

Literature classes are excellent settings for teaching about women-identified cultural traditions. Selecting writings by women counters the long-standing canon of male artists, poets, and writers. My son's seventh-grade literature book featured a special section on Jade Snow Wong, including excerpts from her writing and photographs of her ceramic art. Wong was, however, one of the few women writers represented in the text, while noticeably less-important literary figures such as James Dickey were given extravagant space. Our literature courses should reflect the growing tradition of women poets and writers, not just include a few casually mentioned examples. If textbooks do not feature a satisfactory selection of women writers, students could be challenged to build their own anthologies that celebrate women in literature.

Interviewing one or more female relatives provides an excellent research opportunity for students to learn about the talents and viewpoints of women who have influenced them. Through interviews and essays with this focus, female and male students can learn more about women's and girls' points of view and deepen their appreciation of women's contributions in their own families.

Women-identified communities that reflect their peers' voices and perspectives have special relevance for girls. Anthologies dedicated to writing by and about girls are becoming more prevalent. *Girls: An Anthology* (Chevat et al. 1996) and *Girl Power: Young Women Speak Out!* (Carlip 1995) are two recent examples, for younger and older adolescents, respectively. Students usually feel more confident writing personal essays after they are introduced to examples from anthologies such as these. For teachers, the new anthology *Millennium Girls* (Inness 1998) focuses on understanding contemporary girls in different cultures around the world. *Girls Ink,* a newsletter, is another professional resource that reports on current research about girls and announces new educational opportunities and programs for girls. Scholars in children's literature are producing more work on girls' coming-of-age literature, and contemporary fiction with adolescent heroines offers more interesting and fewer stereotyped roles for girls. For a complete listing of such titles, see Chapter 7, "Beyond Anne Frank and Scout: Females in Young Adult Literature." Girls' magazines such as *New Moon* offer features for eight- to twelve-year-olds from international perspectives, and *HUES* magazine, a multicultural girls' magazine, includes self-esteem features and strategies for self-sufficiency focusing on older girls. School libraries can now access new websites dedicated to the empowerment of girls through the American Association of University Women's webpage, <http://www.aauw.org>. These are only a few of the many language arts resources that teachers can use to help girls feel more connected to each other and to give them more opportunities to have their voices heard. For additional resources, see Chapter 12.

Educators and researchers who are concerned about improving the educational climate for girls face the task of evaluating and incorporating into their curricula the abundant teaching materials about girls and women now being produced. With persistence and patience, we can all share the richly rewarding opportunity to produce gender literacy among our students, colleagues, and parents, as well as other education professionals who are dedicated to improving the opportunities for young women in the middle years of schooling.

References

American Association of University Women. 1991. *Shortchanging Girls, Shortchanging America.* Washington, DC: AAUW Educational Foundation.

———. 1992. *The AAUW Report: How Schools Shortchange Girls.* Washington, DC: AAUW Educational Foundation.

———. 1993. *Hostile Hallways: The AAUW Survey on Sexual Harassment in America's Schools.* Washington, DC: AAUW Educational Foundation.

Brumberg, J. J. 1997. *The Body Project: An Intimate History of American Girls.* New York: Random House.

Bunch, C. 1987. *Passionate Politics: Essays 1968–1986.* New York: St. Martin's Press.

Carlip, H. 1995. *Girl Power: Young Women Speak Out!* New York: Warner Books.

Chevat, E., L. Piette, and A. Argabrite, eds. 1997. *Girls: An Anthology.* New York: Global City Press.

Cohen, J., and S. Blanc. 1996. *Girls in the Middle: Working to Succeed in School.* Washington, DC: AAUW Educational Foundation.

Donoghue, E. 1997. *Kissing the Witch: Old Tales in New Skins.* New York: HarperCollins.

Ellis, A., and M. Llewellyn. 1997. *Dealing with Differences: Taking Action on Class, Race, Gender, and Disability.* Thousand Oaks, CA: Corwin Press.

Girls Ink: A Quarterly Newsletter About Girls Incorporated Programs, Research, and Advocacy. New York: Girls Incorporated.

Henrion, C. 1997. *Women in Mathematics: The Addition of Difference.* Bloomington and Indianapolis: Indiana University Press.

Horgan, D. D. 1995. *Achieving Gender Equity: Strategies for the Classroom.* Boston: Allyn and Bacon.

HUES (Hear Us Emerging Sisters): A Young Woman's Guide to Power and Attitude. Duluth, MN: New Moon Publishing.

Inness, S. 1998. *Millennium Girls: Today's Girls Around the World.* New York: Rowman & Littlefield.

Keller, E. F. 1985. *Reflections on Gender and Science.* New Haven, CT: Yale University Press.

Lakoff, R. 1975. *Language and Woman's Place.* New York: Harper and Row.

Lerner, G. 1986. *The Creation of Patriarchy.* New York: Oxford University Press.

———. 1993. *The Creation of Feminist Consciousness: From the Middle Ages to Eighteen-Seventy.* New York: Oxford University Press.

Lunardini, C. 1997. *What Every American Should Know About Women's History: 200 Events That Shaped Our Destiny.* Holbrook, MA: Adams Media Corporation.

National Women's History Project. 1999. *Women's History Catalog.* Windsor, CA: National Women's History Project.

New Moon: The Magazine for Girls and Their Dreams. Duluth, MN: New Moon Publishing.

Orenstein, P. 1994. *School Girls: Young Women, Self-Esteem, and the Confidence Gap.* New York: Doubleday.

Pipher, M. 1994. *Reviving Ophelia: Saving the Selves of Adolescent Girls.* New York: Ballantine Books.

Rosser, S. V. 1986. *Teaching Science and Health from a Feminist Perspective.* New York: Pergamon Press.

———. 1995. *Teaching the Majority: Breaking the Gender Barrier in Science, Mathematics, and Engineering.* New York: Pergamon Press.

———. 1997. *Re-Engineering Female-Friendly Science.* New York: Pergamon Press.

Sadker, M., and D. Sadker. 1994. *Failing at Fairness: How America's Schools Cheat Girls.* New York: Charles Scribner's Sons.

Sandler, B. R., L. A. Silverberg, and R. M. Hall. 1996. *The Chilly Classroom Climate: A Guide to Improve the Education of Women.* Washington, DC: National Association for Women in Education.

Smith, B. 1998. *The Truth That Never Hurts: Writings About Race, Gender, and Freedom.* New Brunswick, NJ: Rutgers University Press.

Spender, D. 1980. *Man Made Language.* London and New York: Routledge and Kegan Paul.

4

Evaluation Brought to Life

Reconceiving Assessment in Classrooms

KATHY SANFORD

At the age of five, girls enter school with a tentative sense of themselves as gendered beings, a construction that has been developed in them since birth by family, daycare, media, and other social influences. Through traditional teaching practices we reinforce and promote gender constructions. We continually give more attention to those who speak out or act out (predominantly boys). We continue to emphasize mathematics, science, and technology as the important subjects to study; to value analytical thinking; to create black/white, right/wrong dichotomies; and to encourage single perspectives. We focus on male-dominated activities, such as floor hockey or baseball, where competition is encouraged. And we evaluate academic performance in ways that suggest there is one winner, or one right answer that is owned by the authority. Female students have been socialized to accept this traditional understanding of education, to "know their place" and not to question the patriarchal voice of authority that is their teacher's.

To counter these practices and to enable our female students to experience a more positive and growing sense of self-worth and self-identity, many of us have adopted a feminist pedagogy, one that values multiple voices; choice; subjective knowing; and creative and critical thinking. With such an approach to teaching, we can offer different perspectives and strategies through which to understand and construct gender. We can challenge the power hierarchy that has traditionally privileged received knowledge (Belenky et al. 1986). We can provide the space—physical, emotional, spiritual, and mental—that enables multiple perspectives and unique voices to be acknowledged. And we can replace classroom authoritarianism with the informal language of conversation that enables us to construct changing perspectives and perceptions.

41

Too often, however, egalitarian feminist teaching principles are obstructed and sabotaged by the traditional student-assessment strategies used in many classrooms today. Strategies such as exams, critical essays, and end-of-chapter questions support and perpetuate a firmly entrenched patriarchal model of education, one that positions the teacher as dominant authority. Upon reflection, I realized that my own evaluation processes inadvertently mirrored the same patriarchal ways of knowing that feminist pedagogy seeks to disrupt. Despite my attempts to "allow" students to express their views, make choices, take risks, and explore alternative styles, as the teacher, I still held the ultimate power to declare the students' efforts successful or unsuccessful, to open doors for future development or to close them soundly. I have come to see that—despite the rhetoric about the purposes of evaluation (correcting errors, reinforcing previous teaching, giving feedback)—virtually all teacher-generated evaluation is designed to promote competition and to rank the positions of individual students within the educational system.

Recognizing the disjunction between feminist teaching and traditional assessment practices, I was eager to try using evaluative approaches that focused elsewhere, that extended learning processes rather than merely judging them. I wanted to reconfigure the power structures in the classroom and to assess in ways that acknowledged vitality of spirit in learning, encouraged students to develop their own voices without fear of sanction, and allowed me to really hear what students were saying. I recently began teaching in a newly developed program for girls only, which afforded me opportunities to structure alternative teaching and evaluating strategies. My teaching assignment for the year included language arts and social studies (combined as humanities), working with a class of eighth-grade female students, and a complementary drama class for three different classes of seventh- and eighth-grade girls.

I looked for approaches to communicate with my students about their learning development in ways that were individualistic, positive, supportive, and valued by the students, the administrators in the system, and the parents. I realized that there would be skepticism on the part of these interest groups as I changed the traditional "marking" system from one of judging and ranking to one of negotiation and self-assessment. I attempted to prepare my students and myself for discussions that would challenge this alternative approach. The activities and assessment strategies I implemented encouraged the girls to be reflective and articulate about their learning and their ideas.

Peer Assessment and Self-Assessment

Two important activities in which the girls engaged at the beginning of the year were a self-selected reading program, supported by journal writing, and an assignment in which the students were to write a biography of one of their classmates. Both of these activities included various forms of talk, such as interviewing, checking for information, sharing stories, posing questions, and musing aloud. The girls were encouraged to talk to each other and to share their ideas in both oral and written form. The sharing aspect of the classroom became more and more important as the year progressed, as the girls went from needing to be urged to share their work to valuing the opportunity to read and respond to their colleagues' work.

Journal writing was central to the girls' development as articulate and reflective learners. I was aware of the possibility that students, eager to determine "what the teacher wanted," might attempt to manipulate their journal entries to please me rather than pursuing their own ideas and questions. I believed, however, that after the students and I had developed trusting relationships, journals could be a place for establishing connections and relationships between ideas and people. The journals supported my language arts program, in which I implemented a reading workshop, using self-selected reading, and a writing workshop, featuring self-selected writing ideas and formats. The students wrote daily journal entries about their reading and writing and informally shared their journals regularly with me and with their peers. This structure provided opportunities for regular conversations about each student's individual reading and writing, as well as chances for the girls to learn from each other's ideas.

As a class, we discussed possible directions for the journal entries, and together came up with a short collection of possibilities. The list of possible responses (Figure 1) was made into a poster and displayed on the bulletin board for the students' reference. However, the girls knew that they were in no way obliged to use the list if they had other ideas, and many of them never had the need or desire to use it.

I collected the students' journals every other week to read and respond to their ideas. I would jot comments in the margins, on the backs of pages, or wherever else there was room. These comments were not intended to be evaluative in any way, and they often took the form of questions, connections to other books, personal memories, or suggestions for possibilities to consider in future journal entries. I endeavored to develop a written conversation with each student through my comments, and the girls sometimes extended the conversation by responding to my notes. I attempted to keep the evaluative comments completely separate from the conversational ones. To

---

Journal Responses

- discuss the title, cover of the book
- relate the story to personal experiences
- predictions; what will happen next
- personal reactions and feelings about the story
- relating to characters
- clarifying meanings (words, ideas, plot development, etc.)
- discussing language, style, and form of writing
- questions about character motivation; what would I do?
- discuss type of genres (e.g., why science fiction and not realism?)

Figure 1 *Possible Journal Response List Generated by Students*

Journal

Date _____

Comments:

_____

_____

_____

_____

_____

Superior   Acceptable   Incomplete

Figure 2 *Journal Assessment Sheet*

record evaluative comments, I devised a short form that was stapled to the final page of journal responses, as seen in Figure 2. This slip of colored paper provided an easily visible marker between the weeks the journals were collected. The girls were easily able to refer back to previous sections or comments to track their progress and to follow up on suggestions that I had given them.

I initially developed three categories of development—"superior," "acceptable," and "incomplete"—attempting to find descriptors that students could understand and see as attainable for themselves. I avoided any mention of failure because I believed that it was important to the girls to realize that each one of them could be successful in her work. Later in the year, I recognized the need for the girls to have a greater understanding of the descriptors I had selected and to take ownership of them. I then explained my reasons for selecting these terms, and invited the students to develop a set of criteria for each of the categories.

The students' journals developed into personal texts that they could reread; in doing so, they could recognize their own personal changes and development. These journals eventually became a source of information that the girls could use to examine their reading and writing processes and progress.

Exploring Self and Other

The first formal writing activity for the year was a biography assignment that enabled the students to become better acquainted with each other. As this was the beginning of the school year, the students did not know each other well, and I did not know any of them. I randomly paired up the girls and asked them to develop interview questions that they could pose to their partners in order to find enough information about their lives to write a brief biography. The girls then switched positions and were interviewed by their partners. The interview process required a considerable amount of thought and resulted in extensive conversations, both in the initial interview situation and in follow-up meetings.

An aspect of the sharing was, of course, evaluative. Once the biographies were completed, the girls were asked to assess the biography that had been written about them as well as their own written work. They formed judgments as they read each other's writing and struggled to express their ideas and opinions articulately. I initially provided assessment sheets such as the one shown in Figure 3 for the students to complete.

This type of assessment, while being somewhat restrictive, offered the girls a focus for their evaluative reading and comments. It also gave me an opportunity to model various types of responses to students' work, as they read the teacher assessment as well as the peer and self-assessments. I responded in ways that would help the students consider their own work and learn the types of responses they could give to their peers in future work. They needed to develop a vocabulary that would not merely rank their peers' work (good, excellent, messy), but that would also enable them to articulate what made the work of a particular quality, and give them ideas that could direct their future writing.

Grade 8 Humanities

Biography

Self/Peer/Teacher Assessment (circle one)

Completeness of Information—key elements in the person's life are included

_____

_____

Superior   Acceptable   Incomplete

Written Expression—clear, good word choice, smooth sentence structure, unique style

_____

_____

Superior   Acceptable   Incomplete

Format of Biography—unique, fits the content, enhances the information

_____

_____

Superior   Acceptable   Incomplete

Visual Presentation—pleasing to the eye, neat, correct spelling, etc., effective title page

_____

_____

Superior   Acceptable   Incomplete

Figure 3 *Sample Assessment Form*

The ability to articulate was valuable not only for the student who received the comments, but also for the student who wrote them. In addition, the development of a common language for discussing each other's work enabled the creation of a community of learners. The students developed a broader understanding of "acceptable" or "superior" work by being able to read the work of their peers; after considering the work of their peers, they could view their own work with new eyes. I also began to withhold my own assessment until the other students' assessments had been completed. It was my hope that the girls would feel less restricted if they were able to express their own ideas first, without the shadow of my "teacher" comments being imposed.

Following the initial biography projects, in which students used classmates as subjects, a second biography project involved the students selecting a female of a different generation (family or friend) to become the subject of their writing. The girls were required to collect information through interviews, conversations, and document research, then to write the biography as if it were an autobiography, thus also examining the issue of perspective.

In an attempt to further open the conversation about learning and evaluation, I invited parents to participate in the learning and assessment discussions. If possible, the students asked one of their parents (or another adult) to complete an assessment on their second biography project, using the same format as that for self-, peer, and teacher assessment. By involving parents in the assessment process, I hoped to introduce a greater level of understanding and collaboration and enable the girls to see that there are multiple ways of reading and responding to a text, especially a text that is personal.

The final biography project was an autobiography. By this time students had remembered a great deal about their own lives, often in specific and minute detail, through talking about others. These memories enriched their writing and enabled them to better appreciate their own stories. Through their research and their writing, the girls came to know themselves and their classmates better; to value their own families' stories and the stories of their peers; and to make connections between themselves and others.

As the girls wrote assessments of their biographies, I was able to see distinct differences between the peer assessments and the self assessments. Although students became very adept at using our common vocabulary, giving examples and suggestions, they were unable to "see" with the same depth of understanding when they viewed their own work. They shaped the vocabulary to justify their work rather than to examine it critically; it was very difficult for them to view their own work objectively.

As the year progressed, the students' conversations dealt more with the content of the writing and less with comparisons among students' rankings.

It was still very difficult, however, for them to distinguish their writing from their fragile selves. As one teacher commented, "The way we write is an expression of ourselves; it's coming out of us. It's incredibly risky to hand over a piece of writing to be examined for its weaknesses," even more so when we already feel vulnerable and our self-identity is impoverished.

Conferences Become Conversations

Discussing student writing, or "conferencing," offered opportunities for students to express their opinions and ask questions about their work. During the first term, I scheduled a meeting with every student to discuss the contents of their workshop portfolios. These portfolios consisted of the students' written and visual work for the term, including all drafts. Students had the opportunity to review the contents of their portfolios and reflect upon their learning. I had planned to spend about ten minutes in conference with each of the students, asking questions similar to the ones suggested by Nancie Atwell:

- What does someone have to do in order to be a good writer?
- What's your best piece of writing this term?
- What makes it best?
- I notice you made this change in content in this piece of writing. Would you be willing to change it back to the way you first wrote it? Why or why not?
- What are your goals for the next term? (What do you want to try to do as a writer?) (1998)

I felt frustrated throughout the conferences, however, for this practice did not seem to support feminist pedagogy in the way I had hoped. The goals of discussing student writing and assignments are valid (e.g., to give students opportunities to talk about their intentions, to get feedback from genuine readers, and to consider possibilities for further writing). These meetings, however, seemed to have become yet another forum for the teacher to make suggestions, offer criticism, and provide explanations for the evaluations that the teacher had given and deemed appropriate. They struck me as yet another aspect of the patriarchal system, adapted from the business world that continues to influence our teaching. There are usually time restrictions on these conferences, which limits the *amount* of talk that can take place. A specific agenda defined by the teacher limits the *type* of talk that can take place. As I had structured them, conferences were teacher-controlled, allowing the students only the opportunity to hear my feedback and to defend their writing.

They perpetuated the power relations that had traditionally been defined by the educational system, with the teacher firmly positioned as authority in the classroom.

Perhaps because the conferences were scheduled immediately before the report card in an attempt to collaboratively develop a mark with the students, the focus of the conference became the assessment that would appear on the report cards. The students spoke candidly about their feelings in connection to their efforts and results until I asked them to suggest a fair assessment for their term's work (in the form of a letter grade). At that point the girls tended to put on rose-colored glasses and extol their own virtues and those of their work. They usually suggested a grade that was high, often, I believe, based on their desire for success rather than the quality of their work. The conversation would then shift to students' defending their selected grade because of their efforts. I would often disagree, attempt to explain why their grade would not be as high as the one they suggested, and then, as we both left the conference disgruntled, wonder why I had asked them in the first place.

Clearly, my attempts to restructure my teaching using principles of feminist pedagogy were not being supported by conferencing. I needed to find ways of talking with the students that enabled a different understanding of the purpose of talking about their writing. I attempted to broaden the alternatives for conferencing by giving the students more openings in the conversations.

I also began to realize the ongoing need for my students and me to develop a vocabulary through which we could talk about our progress and development. I recognized the need to develop a different structure for talking and negotiating with the girls, and in a class discussion asked them to give me feedback on the assessment processes we had been implementing. Some of the comments caused me to reflect:

Daria: I think we should be marking ourselves. Students should do it. It's our work. We know if we can do it better.

Tamara: Yea, but you would just give yourself As, I mean high marks or whatever.

Daria: No I wouldn't. I am honest. You don't know.

Tamara: Sure. (pause) Not everybody would.

Daria: I thought my original work was bad, gave myself low marks, and I think it's worse now.

I recognized that I had not given the students enough credit for genuine interest in their learning, nor had I considered the societal pressures on them. If talk was going to be genuinely part of the learning process, how could conferences be reconceived in our classroom?

Rather than have conferences seen as formal processes linked to report card grades, I decided to structure them more informally. I would chat with girls on a regular basis, during times when the rest of the class was otherwise occupied. Conferences would not focus on evaluation, and would not be led or controlled by the teacher. The students would have equal authority in determining the content and direction of the conference. I also decided to term our meetings "conversations" rather than "conferences," attempting to balance the power and control within the conversation, making it a genuine sharing of ideas and suggestions rather than a teacher-directed discussion of how and where the student could improve.

Teacher Assessment and Examinations: How Do I Know What I Know?

I continued to assess the girls' writing throughout the year, interspersing my assessments with students' peer and self-assessments. I was able to model some of the possible responses to students' work, showing them alternative aspects to consider. After I had modeled responses, they moved away from standard superficial comments about their own and others' writing, such as "good effort," "I liked the story," and "I worked really hard on this story." Instead, they wrote more specific and longer comments, such as, "You should try making predictions and talking about the characters in depth"; "You might enjoy a more challenging book—you could try *The Giver* by Lois Lowry"; and "Could you rewrite the first sentence—it doesn't seem very clear to me."

The sense of collaborative learning became stronger as the year progressed. At all times I was wary, however, of how much I was leading the girls to give me what I wanted. I did not want to suggest through my own comments that these were the types of responses that would please me, but rather that they were possibilities to consider. However, the students sometimes panicked about how well they were doing, remembering the system that had shaped them for eight years. I had to resist the impulse to tell them what I wanted, instead discussing possibilities for their writing. Although I wanted to point out incorrect structures and usage, I did not want to paralyze the students with a continual search for correctness. I also did not want them to rely on me for the answers, but to learn ways of examining their own work. The impulse to merely tell the girls what to do was strong—remained strong—as it had been long ingrained in my teaching practice. I struggled to learn alternative approaches and to apply my newly learned feminist principles when I was discussing and assessing students' work.

The question of tests and exams recurred during the year. The girls wanted to know if there were going to be any. They had all become accustomed to exams in previous years, to tell them what they knew. They were used to exams that controlled their thinking and their behavior. I thought it would be a worthwhile venture to broaden the concept of "examination" for the students, using feminist pedagogy to structure the examination experience.

The first exam involved the students' reading program. I asked the girls to reread their journal entries from the beginning of the year, the text they had themselves created, and then complete an "Examination of Reading" (Figure 4).

The length of responses varied, but averaged one to two pages of discussion about the student's personal reading habits and developments. The following example is Lisa's response:

> I think that my reading habits have changed over the course of a year. I have varied my reading much more than ever before which has made me think a lot more. The beginning of the year was just usually picking out a book for the sake of reading it, but now I am trying to pick books that I think will challenge me because I find them much more fun. I also like books that are more original because otherwise it gets too boring with the basically same plot.

Grade 8 Humanities

Examination of Reading

You have already reread your journals. Use the ideas you got while you were rereading, as well as any that come to you now.

1. Discuss your reading habits during this year. In relation to your (a) types of reading, (b) amount of reading, (c) place of reading, and (d) understanding of reading, do you see any changes to your reading habits?

If so, describe them in relation to the four points mentioned above.

If not, discuss why you have not changed in any of the four points mentioned above.

2. What change(s) do you think it would be desirable to make to your reading habits? Tell why you think so, in as much detail as possible.

Figure 4 *Examination of Reading*

Where you choose to read and understanding what you read are tied together for me. You must choose a place where you can't be bothered or where you won't let yourself be bothered. If I don't do that no matter what I'm reading I won't understand it, which is why I read at school, before going to bed and on the weekends in my favorite chair when it is quiet. These have worked out to what they are as I read more and better books. The improvement has come slowly but at least has come.

I am also reading a lot more than from the beginning of the year. Before it might have taken me a week to read a one hundred page book now it only takes me a few days.

I could improve by spending extra time I have reading instead of watching television or doing something with no purpose. These are quiet times in my room and I could use them. I don't think I would really mind but I have to push myself to get there.

One of the problems I encounter is, when I go to the library, I usually can't find an interesting book for my reading level. The young adults is too young and the adults is so varied I don't know what would be good. The classics are good but after while [sic] you can get used to them. (April 16, 1996)

Other students commented on the amount of reading they had done. (They referred to the table of contents in their journals, where they had recorded their reading throughout the year—"This year I have moved up in my level of reading, from R. L. Stine, to books like *The Celestine Prophecy*.") They noted their growing enjoyment of reading ("It really does make reading easier if you like it"; "The more interested I am in the book helps speed up how quickly I read it"). And they listed the different types of reading they were doing. They also commented on some of their difficulties, such as finding comfortable reading spaces ("I read in my room at home because that's the only place where my brother and sister aren't"). And they mentioned some of the difficulties they had with reading and with understanding their reading ("Because I am a slow reader I can't read as many books as I would like but I do read every night for at least an hour and also at school in class"). They commented on reading strategies they had developed ("Sometimes it's better to read slower because you have more time to think about what you're reading and understand it better"; "If you have trouble looking for new types of books, before you start a book you should read a couple of pages from the middle to see if you like it"). They told of books they would recommend to others.

The Examination of Reading was assessed by peer comments, which I then read along with the responses. Taken together, they gave fuel to many conversations in the class, and offered me insights through which I could guide students in future reading experiences. Comments were often written in the form of a friendly letter, and showed an engagement with the ideas that had been presented and conversation between two readers in a collaborative and supportive way, as shown in the following sample:

Dear Chloe,

I think that your reading level is of a mature and adult way. It's good to have an open mind about books. I feel that you do. But one thing you should do is to read books that are more for your age. Good, funny books are what everyone needs, and your response sounds as if you only read non-fiction, 100% real books. You should have tried to talk more about #2 question. I don't think that you told enough about that. You gave an excellent response to #1, full, easy to understand, and complete. You sound as though your reading skills have improved a lot since the beginning of the year and your [sic] confident about that and the books you read. Good job, Chloe!

From, Alicia

Through this examination of reading, the girls were recognizing their own ideas as legitimate text for further discussion. They became more aware of their reading abilities and concerns, and were also able to give thoughtful and useful feedback to their peers. I was also able to gain valuable insights from the peer responses.

Another examination, one that would assess not only the students' abilities to learn but also my ability to teach, was the Highest Level of Achievement test, an externally developed test given commonly throughout the school system. This exam consisted of two parts—a multiple choice test of reading skills and a writing test—and compared students' abilities to read and write those of with thousands of other students, male and female. As the students had not written these types of tests in my class during the year, I panicked a bit and determined that they needed a discussion on how to write tests. During the course of the discussion, however, I realized my mistake. The girls had written numerous tests of similar types throughout their school careers, as well as several in other classes during the current year. They were test-wise, and had already been amply prepared in that area.

The tests were written; the results determined. There were a few students who scored poorly. However, these students were the same ones who had been identified earlier (and who had identified themselves) through their journals and other assignments as struggling learners. Most of the girls handled the test in an acceptable or superior way. Two girls scored below acceptable grade standards, ten scored at acceptable grade standards, and thirteen scored above grade level. This was a relief to both them and to me. What had made us doubt? I knew that the students were learning throughout the year, developing and growing in their thinking and their writing. What, then, made us fearful after a year's work?

Conclusions

A memorable incident strengthens my belief in the possibilities for life-long and authentic assessment. In preparation for completing first-term report cards, I distributed to each student a sheet of paper showing the projects we had completed in the term and the collective assessment that had been assigned to the work by the student herself, her peers, and the teacher. The assessment sheet helped the students review their learning for the term and reminded them of the assessments they had helped determine for each completed piece of work. Their task was to consider their work to date and to suggest the grade (A, B, C, or D) that they believed indicated their overall level of performance for the term.

Angie received her assessment sheet and examined it carefully. Although she had always been a good student, Angie's work this year showed a new level of maturity. Her assessment levels reflected this maturity and each piece of work except one had reached a superior level. An essay assignment had not reached a superior level, and Angie asked if she could redo the essay. I replied that she could, but that it was not necessary for grade purposes. I suggested that she had already attained "A" standing. The next day I received a thoroughly revised and edited essay—this time completed on the word processor rather than handwritten. It had been considerably extended, the ideas were more fully developed, and the conclusion had changed to show new thinking about the issue. Angie had chosen to take time to improve her work, not for the teacher, not for the grade, but for herself.

Angie's story exemplifies for me the promise of assessments that create opportunities for both teachers and students to respond ethically and to recognize the identity of the student being assessed. Such an approach respects students' desires and allows them to see that their desires make them unique. Self-assessment, supported by assessments from peers, teachers, and family, enables students to take ownership of their writing and develop skills that allow them to make articulate judgments about their own writing and the writing of others. While this is, admittedly, a time-consuming process, the time consideration lessened for me as I saw my students' work becoming more complex and integrative. As the weeks went on, the girls' voices gained strength and control; they were confident in providing harmonic balance rather than either demanding prominence or being willing to be overpowered and hidden.

Through an alternative understanding of assessment, my students and I openly acknowledged the important force of evaluation and its impact on gender construction. Through collaboration and conversation, we discovered power within and around us, recognizing "self" and "other" as well as the "other" of "self." The authentic relationship with other, suggests Levinas, "is discourse and more exactly, response or responsibility" (1979, 88). Discourse enables multiple voices to exist simultaneously, and acknowledging multiple versions of self has opened spaces in which many voices might sound.

Examining my teaching and assessment practices has also caused me to reflect upon myself. I have attempted to model self-assessment in my classroom, considering alternative lesson plans, strategies, and materials with my students rather than on my own. My previously unquestioned authority has been examined as students have taken on the responsibility of their own assessment. And although initially frightening, the overall experience enabled all of us in the classroom to grow and appreciate each other. Through reversing binaries, privileging what hadn't previously been privileged, we were able to the acknowledge and acclaim our unique value. We came to appreciate how, by reconceiving assessment in the classroom, young women can be offered opportunities to develop a sense of gendered self that is positive, confident, and voiced—and along with it the ability to live fully in a multifaceted and complex world.

References

Atwell, N. 1998. *In the Middle: Writing, Reading, and Learning with Adolescents.* 2d ed. Portsmouth, NH: Heinemann, Boynton-Cook.

Belenky, M., B. Clinchy, N. Goldberger, and J. Tarule. 1986. *Women's Ways of Knowing: The Development of Self, Voice, and Mind.* New York: Basic Books.

Levinas, E. 1979. *Ethics and Infinity.* Pittsburgh: Duquesne University Press.

5

A Net of Relationships

Gender Issues 101

ALICE CROSS AND GERALDINE O'NEILL

We began small. Three women faculty members, fueled by the testimony of Anita Hill, met informally during the spring of 1992 to discuss the status of women and girls at our high school. Were women's voices heard on campus? Were young girls as attended to in and out of the classroom as their male counterparts? Our discussions attracted the attention of other women faculty members and, finally, the principal, who agreed to create a core group of five women, each of whom was to ask one other female teacher to join us to discuss gender issues on campus. At the same time, some faculty members asked for reading material. We created a list of books and articles, and a small coterie of teachers met three times during the summer to discuss what we had read and to consider its place in our lives, both as women and as teachers.

This flurry of activity did not go unnoticed by male faculty members. A few of them questioned our intentions. Some, we won over. The advisor to the student government, for example, upon seeing that we were not male-bashing, joined the group. Later, he helped students draft a statement on harassment to go into the student handbook. Other staff members, however, remained quietly hostile. Nonetheless, the waters were flowing, and all of those small streams converged into a course on gender issues, on which eleven of us collaborated during the fall semester of 1993.

According to Peggy McIntosh (1983), there are several distinct phases in the development of gender-fair curricular "re-vision:"

- Note that there are no women in the curriculum.
- Compensate for that absence by including the select few, always seen in terms of male accomplishments: the female Shakespeare, the female Darwin.
- Discuss women as an oppressed group within a larger, dominant culture.

At this point, the curriculum begins to appear unsatisfactory, and a new way of thinking about the topic, beyond the established order of things, begins to emerge. This is exactly what we decided to do: to step outside the traditional framework of secondary education and see what we could do to bring gender issues into the curriculum in a rich and meaningful way.

Located in a predominantly upper-middle-class suburban community north of New York City, Horace Greeley High School has been cited as one of the top American high schools. More than 95 percent of the students go on to enroll in four-year universities, and many go on to graduate studies. The high school program has a strong liberal arts component supplemented by extensive offerings in music, art, and theater. Although the school is a wonderful place for students to learn, its offerings and conservatively progressive educational philosophy are those of many good suburban high schools, so we had no real model for anything radical, only our own education and our own passion for the subject. The initial group consisted of eight teachers representing six departments: English, science, social studies, foreign language, guidance, and child development. Two more foreign language teachers and a math teacher joined the team later, bringing the total to eleven. Having decided that a team-taught, cross-disciplinary course would address our concerns about gender, we met before school closed in June 1993 to map out a syllabus, so individual team members could spend some time over the summer preparing for the segment that they would teach. We met again in late August to complete the syllabus and to map out common strategies for classroom management and bookkeeping. We agreed to keep a journal that would be passed from teacher to teacher as the semester progressed, so that once a segment was completed, the teacher would make an entry evaluating the segment in light of both student and personal reactions to the topic presented. We also agreed to keep a common grade book throughout the course, and to distribute copies of handouts any one of us used to the ten other members of the team. Each teacher would responsible for assigning and grading at least one activity (a paper, journal entry, test, or presentation) for the segment that he or she presented. We decided that, in lieu of writing a final exam, each student would do a project. We would each serve as a mentor for two or three students to help them through the process.

One of our most serious concerns at first was how to maintain continuity in such a fragmented structure. Eleven teachers moving in and out of a classroom over a twenty-week period seemed chaotic. How would we ever keep track of what was going on, who had said what, what had been discussed, and what had been overlooked? As it worked out, this "chaos" proved to be one of the most exciting elements of the course. The class met at a time when many of us happened to be free. We decided that we would sit in on the presentations as often as possible, at least one in every four class meetings. If one of us were teaching another class at the time Gender Issues met, one of the other teachers would take that class. Sometimes another teacher from the same department would volunteer to step in for a day or two to free her or his colleague. What an exhilarating and educational experience for each of us, to be able to participate as equals in a class with twenty-three tenth through twelfth graders, and to observe colleagues perform their own special kind of classroom magic. Many of us never missed a class!

As we prepared the syllabus for the course, we tried to work in a logical framework from the known to the unknown. We started out with three questions. We posted them in the front of the classroom and each of us referred to them as we worked through our own segment.

- Who are we?
- How have we come to be who we are?
- What changes can we envision (for ourselves and for society) based on what we have learned about ourselves and about the world during this course?

The class was scheduled to meet four times per six-day cycle, and each of us took responsibility for from four to six class meetings. A description of the course and its units follows. (Addendum I contains a complete syllabus.)

GENDER ISSUES FOR THE TWENTY-FIRST CENTURY

This course will focus on topics in which gender creates differences. The following units will be presented by teachers from departments across the curriculum: learning style differences in young children, including the role of heredity versus social conditioning in developing an identity; gender differences in relational skills and how they develop an image of self; images of women in advertising and music videos, and how they reinforce archetypal notions of women and men; biases in science and math education that create different expectations of achievement in these related fields; women and old age, and what it means to grow old and subsequently useless in the role created by society; cultural stereotypes and how they are presented and preserved in different societies; how language reflects social expectations in unconscious but revealing patterns of everyday communication; biological differences between women and men relating to developmental, health, or disease differences; women in the workforce coping with the dual responsibilities of family and profession. Students will study these and other questions both from a theoretical point of view and with research projects. They will design, develop, and carry out such projects in the course of the semester.

COURSE UNITS

Who Are We? How Have We Come to Be Who We Are?

Biological Differences, taught by a science teacher, examined the genetic and biological foundations for our identities as males or females.

Gender Identification, taught by our child-development specialist, studied the development of gender identity and sexism in preschool children.

Educational Biases, shaped by a member of the math department, examined the educational gap between males and females.

Images of Women in Advertising and Music Videos, taught by an English teacher, asked students to raise their awareness of the content and power of the gender messages conveyed in subtle and not-so-subtle ways through mass media.

Media's Influence on Adolescents' Self-Esteem and Body Image, led by the school psychologist, continued the investigation of the media's role in human development.

Adolescence and Coming of Age was a personal essay and dramatic monologue unit in which students could reflect on what they had learned.

What Changes Can We Envision (for Ourselves and Society) Based on What We Have Learned About Ourselves and the World?

Women in the Developing World, taught by a social studies teacher, looked at the plight of women in Third World nations.

Women in the Literature of the Developing World, taught by a French teacher, asked students to consider gender stereotypes in different cultures as they read short works from Africa, Japan, and Latin America.

For Better or Worse: Women and Men in Relationships, team-taught by an English and a Spanish teacher, explored long-term commitments, both heterosexual and homosexual.

Balancing a Career and Family, taught by a Spanish teacher who has done this juggling for years, asked students to think about the gender issues in family life, particularly for the working mother.

Gender Issues 101 originally attracted twenty-three students, six of whom were male. This enrollment prompted an observation in the October 1993 issue of the student newspaper, the *Advocate,* that "Hopefully in the future males won't shy away from such a great opportunity to learn about themselves and members of the opposite sex." The course was offered as an elective and could also be used to fulfill distribution credits for either English or social studies with supplementary work supervised by a member of the selected department. Only three students chose this option, and all selected English. Although the course was primarily designed for juniors and seniors, some sophomores enrolled with special permission.

The projects that students pursued were to be inspired by the classroom readings and discussion, but took a variety of forms:

- a program for cable TV
- a visual display, a performance piece, or photo essay
- an exploration of gender issues in a middle or elementary school
- a short story with a gender issues theme
- research, gathering information and statistics about a particular issue
- a dramatic interpretation of a historical figure or moment in gender-related topics

As we had hoped, students chose a wide range of topics. Some were empirical studies, such as that of a sophomore boy who wrote in his project proposal that he wanted to compare the existence of gender bias in a sixth-grade and a tenth-grade class by looking at who's called on, who's reprimanded, and how students act. His hypothesis was that the evidence of bias would increase as the years went on. Several students selected a more creative approach to their topic. For example, one created a play featuring dialogue among three generations of women in her family about the place of women in the home and the workplace, while another wrote an epilogue to one of the required readings.

Time was devoted to classroom presentations where appropriate, although most projects were submitted in written form. Each project was evaluated by the student's mentor teacher. Overall, we felt quite proud of the course and of the students' enthusiastic engagement with the subject matter. Certainly, there were things we would have altered had we done the class a second time. That there were eleven of us created a few problems. Students could see that no one in particular was in charge. Who exactly should address the talkers in the back of the room? Who called home when papers were late over a period of time, stretching beyond one or two teachers' units? We were not consistent or clear on such issues ourselves.

There were a few pedagogical problems as well. Belenky et al. (1986) suggest that cooperative learning is better for female students than is traditional teacher-centered instruction. However, our short units, with their built-in time constraints, allowed little time for small-group work or for long-term projects cooperatively done. On the other hand, the fact that we teachers sat in on each other's classes, that we participated along with the students, meant that teamwork was woven into the very fabric of the course. The eleven of us had worked together, had learned from and supported each other, and had created and implemented a course without any kind of top-down framework. We created a different kind of learning experience, both for ourselves and for our students.

We would have liked to have had more experiential learning in the course—more studying of small children, more gathering data from students' own classes and life experiences—so that students could see the application of what they were studying in their own lives. And although this kind of learning was limited to their final projects, we saw over the next few years an extension of this kind of awareness in other aspects of school life and student behavior:

- There were articles about equity in sports in the student newspapers.
- Three students in the science research program gathered data comparing the numbers of male and female interactions with teachers during their classes.
- Several students, sponsored by one of the teachers of the Gender Issues course, founded a Gender Issues club whose goal was to educate the student body about issues of harassment and equity.
- One graduate of the Gender Issues class wrote to neighboring schools to see how many, and which, titles they had by women authors, then compared those lists to the works taught in our school.
- Another student, whose project during the Gender Issues course was a study of images of masculinity, went on to do a larger study of student attitudes toward gays and lesbians during his senior year.

Even at the administrative level, we could see some changes. One of the assistant principals made it his policy to shape one of his three classroom observations for each teacher around gender equity. Teachers were regularly informed about whom they had called on first and whether boys and girls were asked the same level of questions, whether there was longer wait time for boys than girls, and so on, issues that pose problems for even the most well-intentioned teachers (Maher 1985).

It would seem we were a resounding success. Well, the story is not quite over: One thing we have not yet noted is that the eleven of us taught this course beyond our regular teaching assignments. Although there had been talk early in our planning about being given relief from our extra assignments (cafeteria, clinic duty, etc.) during the time we were teaching, in fact, this was never done, unfortunately. Our union approached us to remind us that what we were doing could set a terrible precedent: If we could teach an extra class for nothing, why not increase everyone's teaching load the next year? We understood the dangers and agreed that after this semester, we would make changes so that we did not create long-term problems for staff.

The course attracted a lot of attention from the local press, including the *New York Times*. The superintendent, assistant superintendent, and high school principal were all interviewed. All had praise for what we were doing. We were all committed to teaching Gender Issues a second time and had a full section for fall 1994. We also attempted to renegotiate the terms of our elective: Ten of us were willing to give up our free time to teach our units and to mentor students, while the eleventh would have the course officially listed as part of her or his class load.

However, our plans were thwarted in several ways. The biggest villain was the terrible winter in the Northeast that, for two months, caused cancellations or early dismissals every few days. We had never been a high priority with the principal, and as appointments were scheduled and rescheduled, we moved further and further down his list of issues to address. In a subsequent semester, we would undoubtedly have had the assistant superintendent's clear support and attention, but during this, her first year, she had little time for us. In addition, as a leaderless body by choice, one that had only worked in concert, we proved clumsy at fighting for our survival. We had little free time in common to gather with administrators, and we never worked out clearly among ourselves just which teacher or department would claim the course, or what ramifications making that claim would have in terms of assignments, grades, and the like.

In the end, we were unable to resolve the assignment and scheduling difficulties, and the second offering of Gender Issues was canceled. As the years went on, one of the teachers in our group retired, another left the district, a third went on maternity leave; as we dwindled in number and time passed, we lost the will to fight for the elective and instead found other, simpler ways to integrate gender studies into the curriculum. While those of us who remained at the school were careful to keep these issues alive in our classrooms, something was lost by our working only within our own disciplines. The concept of a large group of teachers working together to develop and teach a theme that cuts across all disciplines and affects everyone is at the heart of sound feminist pedagogy. It is, as Carolyn Shrewsbury defines the concept, "A classroom characterized as persons connected in a net of relationships with people who care about each other's learning as well as their own" (1987, 6). This model of teaching calls on everyone involved to perceive both structure and process in a different way, to break the boundaries of traditional thought, and to venture into strategies still untested.

Did we fail? We do not think so. Did we succeed? Not entirely. It takes time to see and then grapple with the problems presented by any new group dynamic. What would have helped us most is a weekly common planning time. This simple accommodation would have afforded us time to talk through difficulties with students, to review our common grade book for gaps, and to collaborate even more fully.

With the passing of time, other ideas for improving the course have emerged. For example, increasing Internet access could allow students to post their final projects on the web, or to attach their findings to the school's webpage, thus making their research available for the benefits of others. Computer chat rooms might allow for dialogue with people not in the course (staff as well as students) or for discussions of issues that there wasn't enough time to explore during class. Perhaps we needed this hiatus to give us time to re-adjust our thinking and to grapple with the real problems that the structure presented. A new school administration, renewed community interest in gender issues, and a different faculty may make the difference.

Addenda

I. Gender Issues Outline/Guide

Unit 1: Biological Differences (9/8 to 9/15; 9/20 to 9/27) Ms. Peters

The course will begin by examining the differences between males and females. The first unit will be divided into five major topics:

a. genetic determination of sex
b. developmental differences—fetal, childhood, puberty, and adulthood
c. reproductive differences
d. neurological differences
e. gender: is it neurological or cultural?

Unit 2: Gender Identification (9/28 to 10/5) Ms. Williams

What are little boys and little girls made of? In this segment the class will look at the facts and fallacies behind stereotypes and nursery rhymes. We will explore the development of gender identity and sexism through readings and observations of preschool children. Discussions and readings will also investigate how and when children learn male and female behavior, as well as how and why gender stereotypes are perpetuated. Readings will be taken from the following:

Boys and Girls: Superheroes in the Doll Corner, Vivian Gussin Paley

"Rethinking the Gender Roles," Susan Gore Zahra

"Sexist Piglets," Irene Pickhardt

"The Gender Factor," Bernice Weissbourd

"Guns and Dolls," Laura Shapiro

"What Are Little Boys and Girls Made Of?" David F. Bjorklund

Unit 3: Educational Biases (10/6 to 10/14) Ms. Clanton

We will look at factors influencing the educational gap between females and males. Do classroom structures favor males? Do females receive less of their teachers' attention? Why is there a lower female enrollment in higher mathematics and science courses in most schools? Even Mattel's Barbie doll has been quoted as saying, "Gee, math class is tough." Why do males score higher on PSATs, and yet females with the same SAT scores get better grades in college? We'll discuss all these questions with an eye toward awareness and change.

Unit 4: Gender Issues in Mass Media: Advertising and Music Videos (10/15 to 10/22; 10/25 to 11/1) Ms. Chadwick

In this unit we will explore two similar forms of mass media: TV advertisements and music videos. We will discuss the defining characteristics of each medium, view and analyze several music videos and TV advertisements, and write, in journal form, about our observations. The purpose of this unit will be to raise our awareness of the content and power of gender messages, which are conveyed in subtle and not-so-subtle ways through these particular forms of mass media. Gender messages communicated through mass media, the similarities between TV advertisements and MTV, the unique and revolutionary characteristics of MTV as a mass medium, some of the criticisms that feminists and others have launched against TV ads and MTV, as well as archetypes and stereotypes, will be discussed. We will also be investigating ways to bring about change in industry and attitudes. Readings will include:

"You've Come a Long Way, Baby . . . or Have You? The Way Advertisers View Women," Samantha Sanderson, *USA Today*

"You've Come a Long Way, Madison Avenue," Betsey Sharkey, *Lears*
Rocking Around the Clock: Music Television, Post Modernism, and
Consumer Culture (excerpt), Ann E. Kaplan

"Music Videos: The Look of the Sound," Pat Aufterheide, *Journal of*
Communication

"Decoding MTV: Values, Views, and Videos," Jeff Kellam, *Media*
and Values

"Sexism on MTV: The Portrayal of Women in Rock Videos,"
Richard C. Vincent, *Journalism Quarterly*

Unit 5: Media's Influence on Adolescents' Self-Esteem and Body Ideal (11/2 to 11/9) Dr. Weinstein

This unit will explore the role that the media plays in influencing the
adolescent perception of beauty and body ideal. The stereotypic characteristics that are perpetuated by the media will be studied. Finally, the
impact that the media has on adolescents' self-perception and self-
esteem will be investigated and gender differences will be noted.

Unit 6: Adolescence and Coming of Age (11/10 to 11/18) Ms. Cross

We'll begin by looking at some personal essays and dramatic mono-
logues, trying on different personas, and speaking in different voices;
then students will experiment with a first-person piece. The writing assignment is loosely focused on identity, on the frustrations/dreams of
the particular person the writer chooses to become (who may or may
not bear a close resemblance to the writer). Students' work may include
media and may even be about their relationship to the media. Models
will be drawn from the following:

> *The Heidi Chronicles,* Wendy Wasserstein
>
> *The House on Mango Street,* Sandra Cisneros
>
> The work of Lynda Barry
>
> "Alice's Restaurant," Arlo Guthrie

Unit 7: Women in the Developing World (11/22 to 12/10) Mr. Houser

In this segment, we will be reading articles and discussing topics such as
the sex ratio in Third World countries, fertility rates and their implications for women, the productivity of women, governments' value of
women in the workforce, women and Islamic fundamentalism, and

the gender differences in cases of poverty—caring for families and the environment.

Unit 8: Literature and Women in the Literature of the Developing World (12/13 to 12/23) Dr. O'Neill

Flannery O'Connor once noted, "A story is a way to say something that can't be said any other way. . . . You tell a story because a statement would be inadequate." In this segment of the course students will read a novel, a short story, and selected poems by or about women of the Third World. These works deal directly with the dilemmas these women face today: polygamy, genital mutilation, child brides and arranged marriages, and the lack of voice and, consequently, power. Closely related to the section on the role of women in the Third World today, these readings have the added power of the literary word to reveal, to stimulate, and, hopefully, to lead to understanding. Selections will be from the following:

So Long a Letter, Mariama Ba

Nectar in a Sieve, Kamala Markandaya

Second Class Citizen, Buchi Emecheta

Unit 9: For Better or Worse: Women and Men in Relationships (1/3 to 1/13) Ms. Abair and Mr. Warren

This session will begin by watching an hour-long film titled For Better or Worse. This documentary explores four different relationships, three heterosexual and one homosexual, all of which have endured for over fifty years. Among other things, the film raises the following gender-related questions: Are women more monogamous than are men? Do women and men who have spent a lifetime together speak the same language? Do men and women expect different things from partners? In what ways do gender stereotypes determine the ways in which men and women conduct themselves in relationships? Are women "easier to know" than men are? These questions will serve as a starting point from which students can begin to consider the ways in which both they and their peers and parents act (or feel they must act) in relationships. Students will be expected to interview (written or videotaped) an individual or couple as a means of closely examining firsthand how gender influences one's behavior in partnerships.

To enhance the discussion of these issues, students will further explore husband/wife relationships in a few short stories:

"Love," Robert Olen Buter

"Say Yes," Tobias Wolff

"Pygmalion," John Updike

Unit 10: Women: Balancing a Career and Family (1/4 to 1/21)
Ms. Materasso

This aspect of the course will focus on the problems and concerns of those women who are juggling a career and family. Some of the topics covered will be harassment and prejudice on the job, equal division of home responsibilities between the husband and wife, and arranging appropriate daycare for the children. Guest speakers will include fathers on paternity leave and an executive, full-time working mother of three children.

II. Those Who Helped to Create Change at Our School

The teachers who were involved in the earliest meetings and in gathering materials: Peggy Breen, Elise Chadwick, Alice Cross, Sue Peters.

The assistant principal who made it his business to see that we gave a fair shake to both girls and boys in the classroom: Larry Breen.

The teachers who advised the student Gender Issues Club: Elise Chadwick, Andrew Selesnick.

III. Summer Reading List: Our Self-Education on Gender Issues

AAUW Report: How Schools Shortchange Girls. 1992. Washington, DC: American Association of University Women Educational Foundation.

Belenky, M., B. Clinchy, N. Goldberger, and J. Tarule. 1986. *Women's Ways of Knowing: The Development of Self, Voice, and Mind.* New York: Basic Books.

Faludi, S. 1991. *Backlash: The Undeclared War Against American Women.* New York: Crown Publishers.

Gilligan, C. 1982. *In a Different Voice: Psychological Theory and Women's Development.* Cambridge, MA: Harvard University Press.

Shakeshaft, C. 1986. "A Gender at Risk." *Phi Delta Kappan* (March): 180–84.

Tavris, Carol. 1993. *The Mismeasure of Women.* New York: Touchstone Books.

Wolff, Naomi. 1992. *The Beauty Myth: How Images of Beauty Are Held Against Women.* New York: Anchor.

References

Belenky, M., B. Clinchy, N. Goldberger, and J. Tarule. 1986. *Women's Ways of Knowing: The Development of Self, Voice, and Mind.* New York: Basic Books.

Maher, F. 1985. "Classroom Pedagogy and the New Scholarship on Women." In *Gendered Subjects,* edited by M. Culley and K. Portuges. New York: Routledge and Kegan Paul.

McIntosh, P. 1983. *Interactive Phases of Curricular Re-Vision: A Feminist Perspective.* Wellesley, MA: Wellesley College Center for Research on Women.

Shrewsbury, C. 1987. "What Is Feminist Pedagogy?" *Women's Studies Quarterly* 15: 7–14.

PART III

Adolescent Girls as Readers

I was a reader and I remember the trouble I had with misogynistic writers. I loved Tolstoy, but it broke my heart to realize when I read The Kreutzer Sonata *that he detested women. Later I had the same experience with Shopenhauer, Henry Miller and Norman Mailer. My daughter, Sara, read Aristotle in her philosophy class. One night she read a section aloud to me and said, "This guy doesn't respect women." I wondered what it means to her that one of the wisest men of the ages is misogynistic.*

—MARY PIPHER, *Reviving Ophelia*

6

Alice, Lolita, *and Me*

Learning to Read "Feminist"
with a Tenth-Grade Urban Adolescent

DEBORAH APPLEMAN

We don't know what women's vision is. What do women's eyes see? How do they carve, invent, decipher the world? I don't know. I know my own vision, the vision of one woman, but the world seen through the eyes of others? I only know what men's eyes see.
—VIVIANE FORRESTER, *New French Feminisms*

Introduction

Is contemporary feminist literary theory relevant to the lives of adolescent girls? With life's other pressing and practical concerns, when even school itself sometimes feels irrelevant, theory may seem too abstract to be either appealing or useful in the adolescent landscape of learning. Yet there is a case to be made for reading with theory, a case that claims that theory can provide agency for students in their own education, a sense of not only reading texts but of reading worlds as well. At an age when students often feel powerless and overwhelmed by authority, theory can help provide them with a sense of control over their meaning making, both in and out of the classroom.

Viviane Forrester's acknowledgment of the limits of her vision and the dominance of men's vision—"what men's eyes see"—provides an explicit rationale for teaching contemporary literary theory, especially feminist literary theory, to adolescents. Theory offers readers critical lenses (Appleman 1992)—perspectives for seeing and reseeing texts through visions that complicate, contradict, or complement our own. Theory also helps us name and recognize the essential quality of other visions: how they shape and inform how we read texts, how we respond to others, how we live our lives. Theory makes the invisible visible, the unsaid said.

Janet Emig argues that the goal of teaching theory is not to make students experts in critical theory, but to encourage them to inhabit theories comfortably enough to construct their own readings and to learn to appreciate the power of multiple perspectives. Emig says that "we must not merely permit, we must actively sponsor those textual and classroom encounters that will allow our students to begin their own odysseys toward their own theoretical maturity" (1990, 94).

Bonnycastle (1991) extends this notion even further, suggesting that the main reason for studying theory at the same time as literature is that it forces the reader to deal consciously with the problem of ideologies. In order to live intelligently in the modern world, one must recognize that there are conflicting ideologies, and that there is no simple direct access to the truth.

It is this perspective, perhaps, that offers the most compelling reason for introducing literary theory to high school students. Learning to view the world from a variety of perspectives and to see differently through the lenses of theory can help adolescents become not only better readers of texts, but better readers of worlds (Appleman 1992; 1993). Literary theory provides not just ways of seeing texts, but ways of analyzing culture as well. This study focuses on the odyssey of Alice, a high school student for whom feminist literary theory provided a way to "decipher the world." (Marks and De Courtivron 1987)

Meeting Alice

This story will surprise those who believe that, if literary theory is taught to secondary students at all, it would be most appropriate only for college preparatory students. I met Alice during her sophomore year when I was teaching a class on multicultural literature at her high school. Alice is the middle child and only daughter in a split family of five. She idolizes her two older brothers, both of whom are still remembered by teachers at her urban Minneapolis high school as being "brilliant" but troubled. Alice's oldest brother is a recovering heroin addict. Alice lives with her two younger brothers and her single mother, a full-time graduate student.

Alice favors the look of studied cast off casualness sported by the "alternative" crowd. Her hair changes color frequently—with a wash, not a dye. Alice has an offbeat kind of fashion flair; she can make Doc Martens work with a dress. Lavender is her favorite color and she sports silver rings on most of her fingers, including her thumbs. As a present to herself, Alice got her tongue pierced on her eighteenth birthday—a decision met with horror by her mother, who considered it a defiling of Alice's natural and honest beauty.

Alice was a remarkably unremarkable student. She moved uncritically through her required reading, wrote nearly illegible essays, hated her journal, and perfected the pout of the reluctant learner. Her classroom participation was regular and sometimes brave, but hardly ever fully engaged. Between independent studies and college classes at the local university, Alice generally managed never to spend an entire day in high school. (Appleman and Hynds 1997, 283)

During her junior year, long after our time in class together was over, Alice asked me if we could do an independent study project as an alternative way of earning her English credits. She said she simply couldn't find any English classes she could tolerate. She seemed restless, unsatisfied, and hungry—for something not on the school menu. When asked what she wanted to study with me, she replied, "Women's studies. I'm not sure what it is, but I think I'd like it."

Alice Meets Theory

Alice and I agreed to meet once a week, at first in the school's library; later we'd leave for coffee shops and pancake houses where Alice would smoke furiously. We began with some general reading in women's studies: introductory chapters from women's studies texts; a variety of pundits' quotations about feminism; and essays by Gloria Steinem, Robin Morgan, Simone de Beauvoir, and others. Together we created the following syllabus:

Alice's Independent Study: Women's Studies

Books

Nonfiction:

Paley, Vivian Gussin. 1984. *Boys and Girls.* Chicago: University of Chicago Press.

Fiction—Choose one:

Walker, Alice. 1992. *The Color Purple.* New York: Harcourt Brace Jovanovich.
Kingsolver, Barbara. 1990. *Animal Dreams.* New York: Harper and Row.
Naylor, Gloria. 1983. *The Women of Brewster Place.* New York: Penguin.

Articles

"X: A Fabulous Child's Story" by Lois Gould from *Issues in Feminism,* Sheila Ruth, ed., Mountain View, CA: Mayfield.

"Know Your Enemy," by Robin Morgan

"Whether Woman Should Have Been Made in the First Production of Things"

"Femininity," by St. Thomas Aquinas

"Women as 'Other,'" by Simone de Beauvoir from *Gender Tales: Tensions in the Schools,* Judith S. Kleinfeld and Suzanne Yerian, eds., New York: St. Martin's Press.

"'Girlspeak' and 'Boyspeak': Gender Differences in Classroom Discussion" by Brenda Weikel.

Short Stories

Glaspell, Susan. 1920. "A Jury of Her Peers." Boston: Small, Maynard & Company.

Gilman, Charlotte Perkins. 1993. "The Yellow Wallpaper." New Brunswick, NJ: Rutgers University Press.

Minot, Susan. 1985. "Lust." In *Growing Up Female,* Susan Cahill, ed., Penguin Group, New York.

Videos

"Killing Me Softly" Dunn

"Thelma and Louise" (1991)

"Heathers" (1989)

Or free choice

Selected Poems

Plays

Sally's Rape. Robbie McCauley. New York: Penumbra.

Requirements

Meet ten times with Professor Appleman.

Discuss nonfiction works and write a one-page reaction for each of three nonfiction works of your choice (a total of three responses).

Write one-page responses to two short stories and three poems (a total of five responses).

Participate in "girl group discussions" on one film.

Participate in "girl group discussions" on play.

Discuss the novel.

Write a two-page essay on the novel.

Final project (may include original writing such as poetry, short story).

Alice's Initial Resistance

Alice quickly displayed a kind of irritation with things labeled feminist. Her working definition of feminism seemed simplistic. For her, feminism was synonymous with anger and a relentless attention to detail. What follows is one of our first exchanges:

D: I want to ask you a question about this one, where it says, "In a sentence or two, please summarize how a feminist reading might change your overall reading of the text." Read what you say here.

A: I'd get pissed. I would bitch a lot and look at every little thing in detail.

D: Tell me more about what you mean by how a feminist would look at every little detail.

A: I think there's, like, different levels of feminism. And, a really strong, hard-core feminist would look at every situation—even walking down the street or standing in line—and look at how men look at her, look at how, um, men talk to her. What they do they look at—her face? Do they look at her boobs, you know?

When they talk to her, you know, if someone, if a guy is waiting in line with her, does the man get waited on first, is the person behind the register more polite to the man or to her?

D: So every little detail kind of becomes more important? And then you would get pissed and bitch a lot. Is that what that level of feminists do?

A: Um, yes. They get angry. I'm not saying they don't have a right to be angry. They have every right in the world to be angry. Women are not treated equally, you know? If I had enough energy to be pissed all the time, I would. I mean, there's tons of things I could find to get pissed about, but that's just not for me, you know? I'm not saying I'm not a feminist, or I'm not as worthy as them or as strong as them or anyone for that matter, but I just don't have the energy to be, to look at every little thing. To me right now, I can't see in my future as I'm going to live, that I am going to be treated equally. I'm not going to have to ever have a man talk to my boobs and not talk to my face, you know?

D: 'Cause you won't let that happen?

A: It does happen. It's not a choice of letting it happen. You can have it happen and scream and bitch at the guy, but it still happens.

D: Right.

A: You know, and if you just want to surround yourself by women, you know, go to stores that only have women that work in them. Walk down the street in a cape, you know, then that's fine, if that's the way you want to live, but it's not for me.

This exchange conveys Alice's initial somewhat paradoxical relationship to theory. On the one hand, she creates a broad caricature of "hard-core" feminists with no sense of humor, who pick at little things. It is an ideology she rejects and wants no part of: "That's fine, if that's the way you want to live, but it's not for me."

On the other hand, Alice articulates some sensibilities about equality and the men's objectification of women that might be labeled feminist. Alice may not want to walk through the Amazonian, "women only" world that she draws out in her last comment, but she doesn't want to be treated as a sex object by men, either. In fact, she will not stand for it: "I'm not going to have to ever have a man talk to my boobs and not talk to my face, you know?"

Alice won't say that she is not a feminist, but because of her negative associations with the term, she is unwilling to say that she is a feminist. On one level, Alice seems to be rejecting what she perceives to be the ideology of feminism, which she finds dogmatic and narrow-minded. Yet her natural sensibilities are strongly feminist, both in terms of her organic belief in the equality and worth of women, and in her ability to detect and name sexism and express her outrage toward it. My goal was to help Alice see how her "vision" was often consonant with the vision of some feminist theorists, who acknowledged her perspective in their writing and offered ways of reading texts to others.

Alice Discovers Her Feminist Lens

One day I asked Alice to respond to some quotations about the status of women from various figures in history. I asked Alice to pick one that struck her particularly and to talk about it. She selected the following, from Napoleon Bonaparte:

Nature intended women to be our slaves . . . they are our property, we are not theirs. They belong to us, just as a tree that bears fruit belongs to a gardener. What a mad ideal to demand equality for women! . . . Women are nothing but machines for producing children.

D: So what do you think of when you read that?

A: Well, the first time I read it, I was actually kind of shocked and mad, and now I read it and think, like, "What a fucking idiot Napoleon is," 'cause what does he think he is, you know?

D: Exactly.

A: What is the whole thing about the tree that bears fruit belongs to a gardener? A tree that bears fruit doesn't belong to anybody.

D: Right.

A: It's just fruit, you know?

D: Right.

A: It belongs to the tree. "Nature intended women to be our slaves." I wonder how he means "nature intended."

D: That that's the way it was meant to be?

A: But, from who? One thing that I've noticed, though, is a lot of these are from the Bible? And that's, like, incredible. How could so many people have such faith in the Bible and they listen to the Bible, when there's all this nasty stuff in it? And who the hell wrote the Bible? That's what I don't understand.

D: But what do you think the gender of whoever wrote the Bible was?

A: It was a man.

D: Yeah. Do you think it's dangerous that all this stuff about women is in the Bible?

A: Yes.

D: Why?

A: So many people look at the Bible as, like, saving them. It's their Bible, you know. They live their life on it. And, if they're going to believe everything that they read in the Bible, check out what they're going to read. With Genesis, this is one quote that I've heard before: "And the rib, which the Lord God had taken from man, made he a woman, and brought her unto the man. And Adam said, 'This is now bone of my bone, and flesh of my flesh: she shall be called Woman, because she was taken out of Man.'" How the hell's a man going to make a woman? There's no way. Women obviously started everything. Men would be nowhere without women. We have babies. We are the ones that can have children, you know? There was a chick first.

D: There was a chick first? And then what?

A: And then, she thought it would be fun to . . . I don't know. All I know is that there was a chick first. I don't know how men got here. Men just evolved out of the sludge in the bottom of the lake.

D: This is reading the Bible through a feminist lens. Right? What if the woman had written the Bible? It would be kind of like that. So, what pisses you off about this quote?

A: About Napoleon, or this one, the Genesis one? (referring to Genesis 2:22–23)

D: Well, are they related in some way?

A: Yes.

D: And what do they share?

A: That women belong to men. Men own women. We owe them everything, we should do whatever we can for men.

D: Do you see women who act like that now?

A: Yeah.

This exchange reveals Alice at her feisty and feminist best. She reveals a spirit and originality of thought I never saw her offer in the open and friendly classroom that we had shared during the fall of her sophomore year. It also underscores a critical aspect that underlay my work with Alice and should, perhaps, underlie all teachers' work with students. As Dewey reminds us, we should shape education to fit the child, rather than shape the child to fit a particular kind of education. Our venture into critical theory did not imbue Alice with any disposition toward feminism that she did not already naturally possess. I was not trying to convert Alice to feminism or have her uncritically adopt a feminist stance in her reading.

What we did try to accomplish in our theoretical journey together was threefold:

1. to broaden Alice's initial narrow definition of feminism; that is, to complicate her somewhat simplistic view of the concept

2. to read writings by women that echoed or underscored Alice's own naturally feminist sentiments and expanded them

3. to apply Alice's elaborated notion of feminism to her reading of literary texts

For example, after this discussion of the Bible, Alice read excerpts from *The Second Sex* (de Beauvoir 1952) and was, in her words, "blown away" to read the following two:

> Thus humanity is male and man defines woman not in herself but as relative to him; she is not regarded as an autonomous being.

> Legislators, priests, philosophers, writers, and scientists have striven to show that the subordinate position of woman is willed in heaven and advantageous on earth.

By articulating her own reaction and then reading feminist criticism, Alice was able to temper her negative predisposition to all things labeled feminist. In addition, she found her own feelings and thoughts to be reinforced and acknowledged as she read them in the words of others.

What Theory Did for Alice

> [W]hether we speak of poets and critics "reading" texts or writers "reading" (and thereby recording for us) the world, we are calling attention to interpretive strategies that are learned, historically determined, and thereby necessarily gender inflected. (Kolodny 1985, 47)

I had selected some short stories for Alice to read, stories frequently cited by feminist critics: "A Jury of Her Peers," by Susan Glaspell, "The Yellow Wallpaper," by Charlotte Perkins, and the less familiar "Lust," by Susan Minot. All three stories invoke, in every aspect of structure, plot, and tone, "the crucial importance of the *sex* of the interpreter" (Kolodny, 55, emphasis hers). We attempted to apply feminist criticism to these works. Again, I was pleasantly surprised by the degree of Alice's engagement with the texts, as well as her ability to read with a feminist lens. Here is an excerpt from our rather lengthy discussion of "A Jury of Her Peers." (See the synopsis of the story in Appendix 2.)

D: What do you notice about, I mean, sort of putting on our feminist lens, our pink eyeglasses here, what do you notice about how, first of all, the men in the story talk to their wives?

A: As if they were imbeciles.

D: Like, can you give me an example? It doesn't have to be word-for-word, but . . .

A: You, oh, you're concerned with the sewing stitches? Ah ha ha ha ha!

D: The trivial things, just kind of a trifle. And what about the women, I mean what kind of references, what kind of rapport develops between the two women, Mrs. Peters and Mrs. Hale?

A: Um, well, at first they don't know each other at all, and then they get, like, a bond, a strong bond, just based on the fact that they're women.

D: And they're in the kitchen, and they're looking at, like, how she keeps her house, and, when they bring her something—do you remember what it is that they're going to bring her?

A: Her apron and her clothes, and her quilt so she doesn't get bored, and I think that's all. Oh, her jar of cherries.

D: And they're going to pretend that they all didn't get . . .

A: Right. Broken.

D: Kind of wrecked. The story starts with Mrs. Hale in the kitchen making cookies or bread or something, and then she has to leave in the middle and there's flour all over. Why do you think the story starts like that?

A: I don't know. I didn't think about that. I don't know. I mean, it could start with what her husband was doing at that moment, when they left, but this is a story about a girl, about women, so. . . . All women's work is woven into the story, even though the story's about murder.

D: So there's this heinous murder in the middle of all this woman's work, of all this housework and stuff like that. So, in the middle there, she and Mrs. Peters develop a bond exactly like you say. Did you find yourself making any guesses about what Mrs. Peters' life must be like with that sheriff?

A: Yeah. Boring. I don't know, always having to be, like, upholding the law or whatever, like how he said, "You marry a sheriff, you marry the law."

D: Let's think about what the title might mean: "A Jury of Her Peers." If you get tried for murder, you're supposed to get tried by a jury of your peers, in other words, people who are basically like you. What do you think the story is trying to say? What if there were twelve men who were her jury?

A: They would not see her side of the story. They wouldn't see. . . . Well, if it was all men who were investigating and all men that were involved in it altogether, they wouldn't know. They'd have no clue what's going on.

D: Right.

A: But if it were all women, then they would understand, and they would give her the lesser sentence. And that's what Mrs. Hale and Mrs. Peters did. They already tried her.

D: Oh, that's really good. I never thought of it that way. They already tried her? And how did they find her?

A: Guilty, but not—shouldn't receive any punishment for it.

D: Extenuating circumstances. It's kind of like—it way prefigures—the battered women syndrome. You know how that's a defense now? And in some ways, even though the story was written a hundred years ago, there's, kind of like, extenuating circumstances. So, would it be too strong to say that in some ways this story is saying that men don't understand women, men can't be women's peers? They don't have a clue?

A: Well, nobody really understanding anybody unless they're, you know, unless they're that person? And, I always think that, well, I just think that women of the same age group, I mean, just people of the same age group and stuff, identify with each other better. I would identify, I would have more things in common with a woman just because I'm a woman than I would with a man.

D: Do you think that your reading of it was any different thinking about feminism, or do you think that thinking about the women would have come out anyway?

A: I think that to some extent I would have already thought about it. But when I'm reading in a feminist lens—it's kind of hard to do in the first place—but, um, it's a lot easier to get offended, and a lot easier to get angry. I guess that's why I don't read with the feminist lens, cause I don't really like to get angry all the time, you know?

D: Is there a way of having the lens make you more aware of things, more sensitive to things, without getting really angry?

A: It can make you sad.

D: Does that say more about the feminist lens, or does that say more about the condition of women and men? I mean, if you get pissed at the men, is that because of the feminist lens, or is that because of how the men are?

A: Because of how the men are. But the feminist lens magnifies it. It makes me see it better. I don't know. It just seems, like, if I'm supposed to read in a feminist lens, I'm supposed to look at every little thing, you know. We examine every little sentence that a woman says and everything that men do. Not really examine, but just, like, just look at it, and, like, how is this woman treated? Why is this woman being treated this way? Which I would see anyway, but I wouldn't spend as much time on.

Alice appears to interpret the story as some feminist theorists have done before her. Alice notices the opposition of male and female realms of meaning and activity (the barn and the kitchen); the automatic bonding of the two women; the denigration of "women's work and worlds." She notes how gendered everything is in the story. She contrasts the men's separateness to the women's closeness, the men's cruelty to the women's kindness, the men's inattention to detail to the women's meticulous attention to everything. This kind of semiotic analysis was expertly done by Kolodny (1985), who uses "A Jury of Her Peers" as a way of demonstrating how women writers play with categories, with "we-ness" and "they-ness," as well as with what she calls "a feminist rereading." Alice read Kolodny's analysis after we had analyzed the story and was approving. She wondered aloud if she had a future as a feminist critic, given her convergence with the published reading. She also pointed out to me the following sentence in *The Second Sex:* "Thus it is that no group ever sets itself up as the One without at once setting up the Other against itself."

In addition, Alice's externalized notion of feminism as anger has begun to soften and give way to sadness. If feminism does more than make you angry, it, as Alice plainly states, "can make you sad." This admission of sadness became especially important as we began to read the novel that Alice had chosen to read next, *Lolita*, by Vladimir Nabokov.

Alice and *Lolita*

I had offered Alice a list of suggested novels to read, including *The Women of Brewster Place*, *The Color Purple*, *The Awakening*, and *Animal Dreams*. Alice said she wanted to read *Lolita* because it was the favorite book of her oldest brother (the recovering addict). At first I felt demoralized. Feminism and *Lolita*? Alice reading *Lolita*? Me having to read it again? I must admit that I briefly considered suggesting an alternative (perhaps a more "politically correct") novel. The thought of wading through Nabokov's seductive prose with sixteen-year-old Alice was not appealing. Then I realized three important things, which in the end most likely served to facilitate Alice's theoretical journey.

First, if reading theory was, ultimately, to be transformative, not just for the way that Alice read texts but for the degree to which she had agency in her own reading and her own learning, then I couldn't interfere in her choices. Second, Alice and I were both motivated by our shared, if unarticulated, sense that she was awash in the sea of traditional schooling, and that she needed an alternative context for learning. If I were going to assign all of her reading, I would be defeating the purpose of our coming together. Third, a feminist lens might be exactly what Alice could use in her reading of Nabokov, perhaps even in her reading of her brother.

We read through the whole novel in a couple of weeks, just reading and talking. Alice kept some notes:

> I like the first paragraph a lot.
> He uses a lot of big words I don't understand.
> It's kind of getting confusing. I think I still like it.

We walked a fine line in our discussion. I tried not to impose any of my own reading of the novel, and to listen to Alice talk it through. Her brother's endorsement of the text had made her response even more complicated. Finally one day she said, "I've got to ask my brother about this book. The women stuff is starting to overwhelm me."

As we applied feminist theory to *Lolita,* Alice's reading of the text began to change. As she read, she began to develop a more acute sense of gender differences in general, as well as a sense of how her femininity and her brother's masculinity played into their reading of *Lolita.* Here are Alice's responses to two questions I posed:

1. What kinds of relationships between men and women are portrayed in the novel? What kinds of generalizations can we make about the relationships between men and women?

   They are unhealthy relationships. The man is in charge, always ruling over the women to get what he wants.

2. How does being a woman affect your reading of the novel? How might your brother's reading be different from yours?

   I notice how women are being treated. I even relate better to the women in the book. My brother would just think it is a good story.

Although Alice still expressed the opinion that feminist critics "look at every little thing," she no longer seemed tied to the notion that feminism was always synonymous with anger. As adults, we recognize both in our lives and in our reading the usefulness of anger as a mask for sadness. Alice, it seemed, was beginning to unmask—a feminist move, perhaps, but in any case, a healthy one.

Using the feminist lens helped Alice learn to take control of her own reading experience. As Schweickart (1986) explains, "Taking control of the reading experience means reading the text as it was not meant to be read, in fact reading it against itself." The notion of resistant reading (Fetterley 1978) is a requisite skill for the female reader, who inevitably encounters predominantly male texts, or even what Culler (1982) called "devious male texts," a label that would surely apply to *Lolita.* Fetterly starkly reminds us that all literature is political and that most literature encountered in American schools is male: "Feminist criticism is a political act whose aim is not simply to interpret the world but to change it, by changing the consciousness of those who read and their relation to what they read" (xxii).

For female readers, learning to read literature means learning to recognize the politics of texts and of our responses to them. In the process of recognizing textual politics and taking a stand with or against the authors and characters, we also begin to articulate a more generalized sense of our places as women who create, out of necessity, feminist readings, not only of texts, but also of worlds.

Conclusion

> ... feminist critical theory is a microcosm of the entire theoretical universe,
> in which a power struggle continues unabated. (Selden 1993, 53)

As Alice's reading became more consciously "gender inflected," she read texts
with a heightened awareness of the power struggle to which Selden alludes—
within texts, within relationships, and within school. For Alice, feminist literary theory provided a means to test and confirm some of her own beliefs, to
disconfirm and challenge other beliefs, and to clarify her own vision of herself and those around her. Alice applied her resistant reading to her assessment of her own education, as well as to the general structure of schools. At
one point she said:

> I think kids can go either way, any way at all, and they just go the way that
> is enforced, you know? I think that kids come out of junior high pretty
> much the same. Then they go to high school and they find their group of
> friends. And there's some groups that study all the time, go to school all the
> time and study all the time, and there are some kids who just go and drop
> out of school. And there are some kids that follow the football team, you
> know, and it's hard to decide why kids go to those different things, you know?
> I don't know. High school is just a bummer, just a bummer. It could be, it
> has so much potential, you know?

Critical theory can provide all students with a way of reading their
worlds; it gives them a different, analytical way of "seeing" that can help them
read culture, the media, and the world around them. Learning to inhabit
multiple ways of knowing can also help students learn to adapt to the intellectual perspectives and learning styles that are required by other disciplines.
Students can see what factors have shaped their own worldviews and what assumptions they make as they evaluate the perspectives of others, whether it's
a character from a text, an author or literary movement, an MTV video, or a
shampoo commercial. Perhaps even more importantly, these skills are needed
in our increasingly diverse classrooms, as we explore the differences between
and among us, and what separates us and what binds us together.

Alice had to stray beyond the traditional boundaries of schooling to be
able to view, as Viviane Forrester states, "the world seen through the eyes
of others." Teacher educators, too, must go beyond the boundaries of traditional literature instruction and find the place of theory in that instruction.
For Alice, feminist literary theory provided a way to make meaning of her
reading, her schooling, and her gendered place in the world. For all the Alices

to follow, may we continue to serve as guides to the kinds of theoretical journeys that will help them learn to find and keep their places in their texts and in their world.

References

Appleman, D. 1992. "I Understood the Grief: Reader Response and Ordinary People." In *Generating Reader's Responses to Literature,* ed. N. Karolides, 92–101. New York: Longman.

————. 1993. "Looking Through Critical Lenses: Teaching Literary Theory to Secondary Students." In *Constructive Reading: Teaching Beyond Communication,* eds. S. Straw and D. Bogdan. Portsmouth: Boynton/Cook.

Appleman, D., and S. Hynds. 1997. "Walking Our Talk: Between Response and Responsibility in the Literature Classroom." *English Education* 29: 283–285.

Bonnycastle, S. 1991. *In Search of Authority: An Introductory Guide to Literary Theory.* Peterborough, Ontario, Canada: Broadview Press.

Culler, J. 1982. "Reading as a Woman" In *Feminisms,* eds. R. R. Warhol and D. P. Herndl, 509–524. New Brunswick, NJ: Rutgers University Press.

de Beauvoir, Simone. 1952. *The Second Sex.* New York: Alfred A. Knopf.

Eagleton, M., ed. 1986. *Feminist Literary Theory: A Reader.* New York: Basil Blackwell.

Emig, J. 1990. "Our Missing Theory". In *Conversations: Contemporary Critical Theory and the Teaching of Literature,* eds. C. Moran and E. F. Penfield, 87–96. Urbana, IL: National Council of Teachers of English.

Fetterley, J. 1978. *The Resisting Reader: A Feminist Approach to American Fiction.* Bloomington: Indiana University Press.

Kolodny, A. 1985. "A Map for Rereading: Gender and the Interpretation of Literary Texts." In *The New Feminist Criticism: Essays on Women, Literature, Theory,* ed. E. Showalter. New York: Pantheon Books.

Marks, E., and I. DeCourtivron. 1987. *New French Feminisms: An Anthology.* New York: Schocken.

Schweickart, P. P. 1986. "Reading Ourselves: Toward a Feminist Theory of Reading." In *Feminisms,* eds. R. R. Warhol and D. P. Herndl, 525–550. New Brunswick, NJ: Rutgers University Press.

Selden, R. 1993. *A Reader's Guide to Contemporary Literary Theory,* 3d ed. New York: Harvester Wheatsheaf.

Appendix 1: Materials Prepared for Alice in Support of Her Reading of *Lolita*

1. What is the feminist lens?

   Feminist literary criticism helps us look at literature in a different light. It applies the philosophies and perspectives of feminism to the literature we read. Feminists like Simone de Beauvoir claim that women have been made inferior and the oppression has been compounded by men's belief that women are inferior by nature (Selden 1993). The abstract notion of "equality" receives lip service, but demands for full equality will usually be resisted. Women themselves, not sympathetic men, are in the best position to assess the true possibilities of womanhood.

   Like feminism itself, feminist literary theory asks us to consider the relationships between men and women, and the roles and status of women in our society. Feminist literary theory assumes that the male-dominated ideology of our culture is reflected in the writing of male authors, which marginalizes women characters as society marginalizes real women.

   There are many different kinds of feminist literary theory. Some theories examine the language and symbols that are used; some look at how the gender of the author affects how things are written; and some look at how the characters, especially the female characters, are portrayed. For example, feminist literary critics look at the portrayal of women characters to expose the patriarchal ideology implicit in many canonical works, showing how clearly the tradition of systematic masculine dominance is inscribed in our literary tradition. This tradition guides how female characters are created to either remain silent or to speak the myths that men would have them speak.

   Feminist literary theory also invites us to pay particular attention to the patterns of thought, behavior, values, and power in relationships. It suggests that the reader's gender often affects the reader's response to a text. Male writers often address their readers as if they were all men and exclude female readers.

   Feminist literary critics remind us that literary values and conventions have themselves been shaped by men, and that gender stereotypes affect how both men and women produce literature.

2. How do we apply the feminist lens?

   We apply it by closely examining the portrayal of the characters (both female and male), the language of the text, the author's attitude, and the relationships between the characters.

3. Applying the feminist lens to *Lolita*

    1. Write a few sentences about how each of the following female characters is portrayed. Think about their physical description, their behavior, and their power or lack of it. What kinds of words are used to describe them? Be specific.

    Annabel:

    Valeria:

    Charlotte:

    Dolores / Lolita:

    2. In a few words, describe Humbert Humbert's attitude toward girls:

    women:

    sex:

    3. What kinds of relationships between men and women are portrayed in the novel? What kinds of generalizations can we make about these relationships between men and women?

    4. From a feminist perspective, what might be troubling about the way in which women and girls are portrayed in the novel?

    5. How does being a woman affect your reading of the novel? How might your brother's reading be different from yours?

    6. In a sentence or two, please summarize how a feminist reading might change your overall reading of the text.

Appendix 2: Synopsis of "A Jury of Her Peers"

Susan Glaspell's "A Jury of Her Peers" is based on her widely anthologized and frequently produced one-act play, *Trifles*. In the story, Mrs. Hale and the sheriff's wife accompany the sheriff and his deputies to the home of a woman accused of murdering her husband. While the suspect, Mrs. Wright, is locked in the town jail, the visitors search her home for clues to what happened and why. Only the women, noticing small things (quilt pieces, a broken stove, fruit jars, a half-dirty dish towel, a broken bird cage, and, finally, in a small box, a dead bird with a broken neck) are able to piece together the motivation of the accused woman. Together, in silent sisterhood, Mrs. Hale and the sheriff's wife conspire to hide any incriminating evidence and collect some items to bring to the suspect in jail, including the dead bird. The men fail to notice what they take, claiming that "women are used to worrying over trifles."

7

Beyond Anne Frank and Scout

Females in Young Adult Literature

JUDITH A. HAYN AND LISA A. SPIEGEL

Contemporary young adult literature reflects the situations, needs, and interests of young people, yet adolescent literature continues to be used mostly in upper-elementary and middle schools with reluctant readers (Christenbury 1993). These novels are still fairly popular in grade nine (38 percent of ninth-grade teachers use young adult literature), but by grade twelve are virtually nonexistent (only 3 percent of teachers select these books for their classes) (Applebee 1989).

Too often, teachers fail to select literature that enables students to become emotionally and cognitively involved in what they read, which results in students reading literature that is inconsistent with their developmental stages and abilities (Bushman and Bushman 1997). Because students are assigned inappropriate novels (i.e., mostly adult classics) that they are unable to interact with, they learn *about* literature rather than learning *from* it.

The classical canon often seems far removed from contemporary students' everyday lives, and not even the most voracious reader will find much insight or enjoyment in reading school texts during the teenage years. Neither will poorer or disinterested readers, who are likely to encounter difficulties with simply reading and understanding these sophisticated and complicated works written for the adults of past centuries.

Young adult literature, however, has the potential for increasing students' understanding of themselves and their lives by offering an opportunity for reading and studying works they enjoy. Because quality adolescent literature is being written for various ages and reading levels, it's possible for every student to become engaged in reading for enjoyment.

Embedded within the general lack of regard for providing engaging, relevant literature to young readers is the shortage of texts that portray girls and women in positive, nonstereotypical ways. Most middle and high school language arts reading lists display plenty of works by and about men, but contain few by and about women. Thus, adolescent literature is important for all students, but especially for girls (Spiegel 1996). Young people need to read and study women because otherwise they see only half a picture of the human race (Whaley and Dodge 1993). When English/language arts teachers include more literature by and about women in their classrooms, they enable both their male and female students to become more knowledgeable, and more compassionate and respectful toward girls and women.

Even as educators work to include texts representative of women and other minorities, the flow of antifeminism and antimulticulturalism articles and books continues. E. D. Hirsch's *Cultural Literacy: What Every American Needs to Know* and Allan Bloom's *The Closing of the American Mind,* along with Dinesh D'Souza's *Illiberal Education: The Politics of Race and Sex on Campus,* push against a more inclusive curriculum. Others equate diversifying the traditional canon with lowering educational standards. The problem is not that classical works are taught in schools; it is the policy of teaching these works to the exclusion of others (Whaley and Dodge 1993).

Students easily hear voices that are similar to their own, but they need assistance to hear voices that are truly unlike their own, to be curious about, and even seek, voices that contradict their worldview or offer experiences they will never have (Whaley and Dodge 1993).

What happens to students who are exposed to sex-equitable material? Students using inclusive materials are more likely than others to have gender-balanced knowledge of people in society, develop more flexible attitudes along with more accurate sex role knowledge, and imitate the role behaviors contained in the materials (Scott and Schau 1985).

Researchers have found that sex roles are learned behaviors; that sex role definitions can be learned from role models, including those in books; and that role definitions that are narrow or rigid can be harmful to development (Purcell and Stewart 1990). There are, indeed, a multitude of benefits to be gained from using inclusive literature in the classroom.

Focusing upon young adult literature that features strong female protagonists validates and strengthens females. It allows males to experience a different perspective and, thus, increase their appreciation of and adjust their attitudes toward women. Both male and female readers need books that reaffirm their own experiences of being adolescent boys and girls, as well as providing them with new challenges, situations, and insights.

When we use a majority of male voices, we deny males (and, of course, females) the chance to understand the concerns and feelings of women (Carlson 1989). It is vital for men to learn more about women. Negative role models that may be presented in curriculum can reinforce old prejudices that prevent a student's ability to see beyond them. Without meaningful role models, males and females will have trouble imagining the kind of women they would admire. Including the experiences and writings of women increases the truths we can discover about life by more than half.

Aiding the classroom teacher in meeting these challenges is the proliferation of many high-quality young adult novels that span a variety of genres and feature strong female characters. Problem novels, where the author places an adolescent female character in a situation where her dilemma becomes a central part of the plot development, are popular choices for teens. In Harper Lee's traditional classroom selection *To Kill a Mockingbird*, Scout comes of age in the Deep South of the 1930s. While young females can identify with Scout's growth and development, selecting a more contemporary heroine's story to pair with it reminds readers that the search for identity is universal. Cynthia Rylant's heroine Summer in *Missing May* and Ruth White's Gypsy in *Belle Prater's Boy* are two similar dynamic characters who, like Scout, bond with young boys who lead them to face their fears and doubts dealing with death and loss as they mature.

By pairing classic young adult books with more recent ones, teachers can lead students to see that the same themes emerge over time through the eyes of many characters, especially those of young girls. In three compelling novels, Bruce Brooks, Sharon Creech, and Han Nolan chronicle the journeys of three teenagers. Sibilance T. Spooner, in *Midnight Hour Encores*, travels with her unconventional father to meet the mother who deserted her at birth; Salamanca Tree Hiddle, in *Walk Two Moons*, leaves Ohio for Idaho with her grandparents in search of her mother; and Charity Pittman, in *Send Me down a Miracle*, plans to follow in her preacher father's footsteps until the summer her mother leaves Casper, Alabama, for good. In another novel dealing with adolescent religious doubts, *Miriam's Well*, Lois Ruby chooses Miriam Pelham as her heroine. When Miriam is diagnosed with cancer, her fundamentalist church's beliefs will not allow medical treatment; the search for a legal solution raises conflicts for all readers.

In adventure and survival tales, males proliferate as protagonists. A well-known, popular classic novel by Jean Craighead George, *Julie of the Wolves*, and its sequel, *Julie*, feature a female survivor. The heroine, who has survived life in the frozen tundra, returns to her Inuit father and her village, only to find that world much changed and threatened by the wolves she loves and understands so well. In more familiar surroundings, Will Hobbs delivers two gripping page-turners featuring Jessie, a female member of a group of societal misfits enrolled in a program called Discovery Unlimited in Colorado. In *Downriver*, the group abandons its counselor-guide and attempts to shoot the Grand Canyon's rapids. Their story continues in the sequel *River Thunder*, in which Jessie and her friends repeat the trip, this time with Al, the adult leader, along for the terrifying ride.

Sometimes the problems encountered by adolescent heroines are graphic, powerful, and disturbing. In *Chinese Handcuffs*, Chris Crutcher explores the issues of abuse and young females through the letters that Dillon Hemingway writes to his brother who has committed suicide. Dillon pursues a relationship with Jennifer Lawless, a star basketball player who reveals her stepfather's molestation as the friendship between the two grows and changes. James Howe casts Margaret as *The Watcher*, who looks to Eric, the narrator of her tale, to help her escape a similar tyranny. Perhaps the most shocking and thought-provoking is the story of Em Thurkill, the heroine of *When She Was Good*; Norma Fox Mazer chronicles her protagonist's struggle to cope with the death of an abusive sister as Em tries to survive while keeping her secrets locked within her. Undoubtedly, these three novels are geared for the mature reader and may be too explicit for whole-class reading, but they could be part of a classroom library.

On the other hand, the often-taught classic *The Pigman*, by Paul Zindel, allows John Conlan and Lorraine Jensen, in alternating points of view, to tell their story of adolescents coming to terms with grief and compassion through friendship with an elderly, grieving man. Jim Heynen explores another unlikely relationship in *Being Youngest*, as Gretchen and Henry, both tormented by their older siblings, form a bond with each other and later a friendship with an eccentric older couple, resulting in lessons of tolerance and compassion.

Historical novels offer another genre for the classroom. A common nonfiction classroom selection is *Anne Frank: The Diary of a Young Girl*, which appears in dramatized form in many anthologies. Finding fictional accounts based on historical events involving adolescent girls leads to an increasing awareness of female viewpoints of the past, viewpoints that are often neglected in history books. In *Number the Stars*, a text that is often used in middle school classrooms, Lois Lowry traces the story of Annemarie Johansen and her friendship with Ellen Rosen, a Jew, in Nazi-occupied Copenhagen. A switch on this theme occurs in Jane Yolen's *The Devil's Arithmetic*, in which Hannah, who lives in the United States in 1988, is suddenly transported in time to become Chaya in a 1942 Polish concentration camp. In *Briar Rose*, Yolen uses the parallel tale of Sleeping Beauty in relating Becca's efforts to uncover her grandmother's past in Poland, as she reclaims her family's heritage.

Patricia Reilly Giff tells in *Lily's Crossing* of one girl's friendship with a young boy who escaped the horrors of war-torn Europe.

World War II is not the only era to provide authors with rich historical settings in which girls may emerge as heroines. Katherine Paterson puts *Lyddie* in the mills of Lowell, Massachusetts, in the early 1800s. Carolyn Meyer sets *White Lilacs,* her coming of age narrative for Rose Lee Jefferson, in 1921 in Freedom, Texas. And Karen Hesse sets her Newberry winner *Out of the Dust* in the 1934–1935 Oklahoma Dust Bowl, where Billie Jo emerges as a triumphant survivor. In *Nightjohn* and its sequel *Sarny,* Gary Paulsen tells the adventures during and after the Civil War of a young slave girl who learns to read.

Noted for her historical novels, Ann Rinaldi's most recent heroine is Emily Bransby Pigbush, the protagonist in *An Acquaintance with Darkness.* Fourteen-year-old Emily loses her mother to tuberculosis shortly after Lincoln's assassination; has her best friend Annie Surratt's mother jailed for the crime of allegedly aiding the plotters; and is forced to live with an uncle, a renowned doctor whom her mother hated. The premise of the novel lies in the ghoulish practices that the emerging medical profession used to gain knowledge of human anatomy. In *Catherine, Called Birdy,* Karen Cushman places her spirited, funny, diary-keeping heroine in 1290 England; her second protagonist is Brat/Beetle, who searches for her place in medieval times with the assumed identity of Alyce in *The Midwife's Apprentice.*

Multicultural literature is also rich in material that has strong female protagonists and is appropriate to middle and secondary classrooms. As Hayn and Sherrill note, "Outside the world literature textbook, where the selections are often difficult to read and seem irrelevant to modern adolescents, the opportunities to engage with texts with this focus are rare" (1997, 43). Readers might come to know something of Hispanic culture from reading Julia Alvarez's *How the Garcia Girls Lost Their Accents,* as they have from Sandra Cisneros' familiar autobiographical novel, *The House on Mango Street.* The first relates the story of the four Garcia sisters, who adjust to immigrant life in New York City after leaving the Dominican Republic. The second tells of Esperanza Cordero, who grows up in the Latino section of Chicago. Edwidge Danticat explores the Haitian female's perspective in the powerful novel *Breath, Eyes, Memory.* Twelve-year-old Sophie Caco, the heroine, is sent from her poverty-stricken native island to New York to be reunited with a barely remembered mother; her return to her past chronicles a portrait of the influences of the supernatural and political upheaval on Haitian women.

Asian cultures also can provide engaging reading experiences for young readers. Suzanne Fisher Staples writes of *Shabanu, Daughter of the Wind* and the arranged marriage of this eleven-year-old girl in Pakistan. This novel is a frequent choice in classroom sets for the middle-level reader; moreover, its sequel, *Haveli,* continues Shabanu's story as she emerges from her role as the youngest wife of Rahim, a wealthy Pakistani landowner, and becomes a young woman of spirit and courage who must make difficult choices.

Amy Tan's *The Joy Luck Club,* which is a popular high school selection, explores the Chinese American experience. Lensey Namioka takes the reader into the world of *April and the Dragon Lady* in contemporary Seattle to reveal the relationship between a young girl and the traditional Chinese grandmother who rules her world. Marie G. Lee's autobiography, *Finding My Voice,* lets readers see the struggles of a Korean American girl, Ellen Sung, growing up in the suburbs of Minnesota as she experiences the trials and tribulations of her senior year in high school, compounded by doubtful feelings about her ethnic identity.

Mildred Taylor's young adult classics featuring Cassie Logan, *Roll of Thunder, Hear My Cry* and *Let the Circle Be Unbroken,* still move and challenge young people. Strong female adolescent African American characters can be found in more recent works, as well. Jacqueline Woodson's *I Hadn't Meant to Tell You This* deals with a reversal of power. Marie is a leader among the popular black girls in Chauncey, Ohio, a prosperous black suburb. She befriends Lena, a poor white student, who moves to town. Both have lost their mothers, and Lena carries a terrible secret about her father. In addition, Woodson has written the Maizon series. In *Maizon at Blue Hill,* her black heroine attends an all-white boarding school, traveling from her Brooklyn neighborhood to Connecticut. This is a sequel to *Between Madison and Palmetto,* in which Maizon's encounter with her heritage begins. In *Plain City,* Virginia Hamilton recounts the story of Buhlaire Simms, an interracial child who struggles with her own identity.

Though efforts to find high-quality multicultural selections with female protagonists can be rewarding, it is not easy to deal with the addiction that young adolescent girls have to series books in three popular genres: romance, mystery/horror, and fantasy/science fiction. The genuinely readable books with realistic situations tend to be overshadowed by the multitude of series books, which are attractively displayed in row after row of vibrant, colorful paperbacks. If R. L. Stine, Christopher Pike, and Francine Pascal entice young readers through glitzy marketing, how can adolescents be persuaded to read books with memorable characters and nonformulaic plots?

With careful guidance, a young reader can be led to award-winning books with the same themes as those gracing teen and pre-teen best-seller lists. Fans can follow the puzzling adventures of Janie in Caroline Cooney's trio about a young girl's discovery that she is not the biological daughter of her parents: *The Face on the Milk Carton, Whatever Happened to Janie?,* and *The*

Voice on the Radio. Cooney also writes convincing vampire tales; one example is *The Cheerleader,* in which a young girl, Althea, bargains for popularity, but loses much more. Annette Curtis Klause moves romance farther into horror in her tale of Vivian Gandillon, who yearns to change, as she must, from girl to wolf. Her turmoil at age sixteen in *Blood and Chocolate* parallels that of the adolescent who wants so much to belong in an alien world and finds the price too high.

Fantasy can be a welcome escape for the teen reader, and Madeleine L'Engle's classic, *A Wrinkle in Time,* relates Meg Murry's imaginative, compelling adventures. Natalie Babbit, in the popular *Tuck Everlasting,* tells of Winnie's discovery in the forest of the gift of eternal life and her subsequent choice between being mortal or immortal. More recent works include Bruce Coville's story of Cara, who, in *Into the Land of the Unicorns* (Book One of Coville's Unicorn Chronicles), jumps off a tower to elude a threatening stranger and lands in Luster. The heroine in Sherwood Smith's *Crown Duel* is Mel, who becomes a countess after the death of her father. Enmeshed in politics and war, Mel is captured by opposition forces, and her journey from captivity to freedom parallels her own coming of age.

Patricia Wrede takes two familiar fairy tale characters, *Snow White and Rose Red* and places them in Elizabethan England, where they are swept up in a plot involving the Queen of Faeries and her two half-mortal sons. In a contemporary selection, Gail Carson Levine retells the familiar Cinderella story. She sets *Ella Enchanted* in a different time and place, in a land filled with ogres, giants, a handsome prince, confused witches, and enough action to keep a reader engrossed until the "happily ever after" ending predictable of this genre.

In addition, quality mystery/suspense can fascinate young readers more thoroughly than can the simplistic plots of less challenging series books. If Lois Duncan's *Killing Mr. Griffin* and *I Know What You Did Last Summer* are classroom free-choice reading staples, other more recent titles can be found to keep the fascination with scary stories alive. Another author of quality mysteries is Joan Lowery Nixon, who, in *The Name of the Game Was Murder* and others, features adolescent girls as detectives. In this page-turner, fifteen-year-old Samantha Burns plots to vacation at the secluded island home of her great-uncle, Augustus Trevor, a famous novelist. Hoping to get his advice on starting her own career in writing, she instead has to solve his murder; his other guests are five celebrities who, along with Samantha's aunt, emerge as suspects.

In *Sharp Horns on the Moon,* Chris Crowe features lonely Ivy, who befriends a ghost; this friendship helps Ivy put her mother's death into perspective and mature as a person. In Vicki Grove's thriller *Rimwalkers,* the main character is Tory, whose summer vacation leads to the search for a young boy, an ancestor of Tory's who drowned in the 1840s in the creek adjacent to her grandparents' farm. The ancestor appears and reappears to Tory and her two cousins. The youngsters find that adolescence is an innocent and vulnerable time, and that one incident can change lives forever.

Science fiction provides young readers with complex, thought-provoking plots, as in Karen Hesse's *The Music of Dolphins.* Feral Mila has been raised by dolphins off the Florida coast; found by researchers, she is taught to be a "human" once more. Readers can witness the pain of this unwanted transformation and question the ethical issues behind it. Ethics are also central to Peter Dickinson's *Eva,* in which a teenage girl's brain is transplanted into a chimp's body as a lifesaving device after a terrible accident. Current societal issues also provide common themes. Robert C. O'Brien's classic *Z for Zachariah* tells the story of a sixteen-year-old girl left alive—and seemingly alone—after a nuclear war, while Karen Hesse's *Phoenix Rising* discusses the effects of a nuclear accident upon its female protagonist and her family.

The adolescent attraction to series books can be dealt with through discriminating suggestions from a well-informed teacher, parent, or librarian. Including topics that might make readers uncomfortable or that challenge traditional value systems, however, can be more difficult. Gay and lesbian protagonists, however, do exist in sensitive, well-crafted portrayals by some of young adult literature's finest authors. A text such as the classic *Ruby,* by Rosa Guy, in which the eighteen-year-old heroine has a lesbian relationship with beautiful Daphne, can serve as a lifeline to a troubled, confused adolescent girl. A more contemporary choice is *Deliver Us from Evie,* by M. E. Kerr. Evie is a lesbian who, though comfortable with herself, does not fit in with her family or the small farming community in which she lives. Told from the viewpoint of her sensitive younger brother, who is still in high school, Evie finds a way to escape and to begin a fulfilling life. Bette Greene uses a heterosexual female protagonist, Carla Wayland, in her award-winning novel, *The Drowning of Stephan Jones,* to relate the horrors of homophobia in a small, conservative Arkansas town. While homosexuality often remains hidden in the classroom, tolerance builds through knowledge, and young adult literature can be an effective teaching tool, just as it is with sexual abuse, abandonment, violence, and suicide.

The texts exist. Female characters of all ages, from all cultures, throughout time, in reality or fantasy populate the young adult novels cited above and many more. Under stultifying and discriminatory conditions, their female characters emerge as heroines, protagonists who conquer typical and unusual conflicts to emerge triumphant. The discerning classroom teacher can and must find texts to extend the traditional "half-view" of the canon and build a set of readings that benefit all students.

Points to Notice/Classroom Use

- Ask "Where are *you* in the story?" (Whaley and Dodge 1993) when reading and discussing with students. Do not assume that all males and females identify with only their same gender, or that characters have gender-specific traits.
- Rather than asking "What's a good book for *females?*" ask, "What's a *good book?*" The best books are not gender-bound. Books that appeal to only one sex may not be the best choice. Do not gender-stereotype males and females.
- Books about or with females do not have to be written by female authors. But weave books about, for, and by women and girls into every aspect of the curriculum, especially materials that show females as active participants in life and as able to succeed in any endeavor, rather than as passive observers and recipients of the actions and decisions of others.
- Examine series books. Why are these books so popular? What qualities of these books appeal to young girls, and why? How do these books contribute to stereotyping the characteristics of their female protagonists?
- Use literature purposefully so readers identify with the characters and understand that the admirable qualities possessed by both male and female characters are qualities that they may wish to emulate in their own lives.
- Pair books with similar themes or topics to include both a male and a female protagonist. For example, when reading survival books like Gary Paulsen's *Hatchet* and *The River,* pair them with those featuring a female main character, such as *Downriver* and *River Thunder* by Will Hobbs.
- Discuss the treatment of characters in a novel. How do girls treat boys? How do boys treat girls? How do adults react with both genders? How does this resemble real life?
- Take a global view of literature by valuing the stories and writing of people from all cultural groups and walks of life.
- Privilege the more feminine styles and forms of writing by asking students to read and write in many formats, including diaries, journals, and dramas.
- Build an understanding of gender roles as affected by cultural mores by pairing titles; for example, pair Staple's *Haveli* with Namioka's *April and the Dragon Lady.*

- Examine the role of gender in the media and analyze the ways in which girls, women, boys, and men may be defined stereotypically. Include nonprint media that present the sexes in positive and nonstereotypical roles.

- Pair a work from the traditional canon, such as *Anne Frank: The Diary of a Young Girl*, with a more recent work that explores similar lives, similar struggles, or a similar era, such as Yolen's *Briar Rose*.

- Use children's literature to help students explore complex issues and themes through illustrations and simplified story lines.

- Implement classroom strategies such as literature circles (Daniels 1994) and response groups to ensure personal engagement with the text's concerns and encourage the voicing of variant opinions.

Adolescent Literature Cited

Alvarez, J. 1992. *How the Garcia Girls Lost Their Accents.* New York: Penguin/Plum Books.

Babbitt, N. 1975. *Tuck Everlasting.* New York: Farrar, Straus & Giroux.

Brooks, B. 1986. *Midnight Hour Encores.* New York: Harper & Row.

Cisneros, S. 1985. *The House on Mango Street.* Houston: Arte Publico Books.

Cooney, C. 1990. *The Face on the Milk Carton.* Des Plaines, IL: Bantam.

———. 1991. *The Cheerleader.* Bergenfield, NJ: Scholastic.

———. 1993. *Whatever Happened to Janie?* New York: Delacorte.

———. 1996. *The Voice on the Radio.* New York: Delacorte.

Coville, B. 1994. *Into the Land of the Unicorns.* New York: Scholastic.

Creech, S. 1994. *Walk Two Moons.* New York: Scholastic.

Crowe, C. 1998. *Sharp Horns on the Moon.* New York: Boyds Mills Press.

Crutcher, C. 1989. *Chinese Handcuffs.* New York: Greenwillow.

Cushman, K. 1994. *Catherine, Called Birdy.* New York: HarperCollins.

———. 1995. *The Midwife's Apprentice.* New York: HarperCollins.

Danticat, E. 1994. *Breath, Eyes, Memory.* New York: Vintage Books.

Dickinson, P. 1989. *Eva.* New York: Delacorte.

Duncan, L. 1973. *I Know What You Did Last Summer.* New York: Simon & Schuster.

———. 1978. *Killing Mr. Griffin.* New York: Simon & Schuster.

Frank, A. 1967. *Anne Frank: The Diary of a Young Girl.* New York: Doubleday.

George, J. C. 1972. *Julie of the Wolves*. New York: Trumpet Club.

———. 1994. *Julie*. New York: HarperCollins.

Giff, P. R. 1997. *Lily's Crossing*. New York: Delacorte.

Greene, B. 1991. *The Drowning of Stephan Jones*. New York: Bantam.

Grove, V. 1993. *Rimwalkers*. New York: Putnam.

Guy, R. 1976. *Ruby*. New York: Dell.

Hamilton, V. 1993. *Plain City*. New York: The Blue Sky Press.

Hesse, K. 1994. *Phoenix Rising*. New York: Henry Holt & Co.

———. 1996. *The Music of Dolphins*. New York: Scholastic.

———. 1997. *Out of the Dust*. New York: Scholastic.

Heynen, J. 1997. *Being Youngest*. New York: Henry Holt.

Hobbs, W. 1991. *Downriver*. New York: Dell.

———. 1997. *River Thunder*. New York: Delacorte.

Howe, J. 1997. *The Watcher*. New York: Atheneum Books.

Kerr, M. E. 1994. *Deliver Us from Evie*. Scranton, PA: HarperCollins.

Klause, A. C. 1997. *Blood and Chocolate*. New York: Delacorte.

Lee, H. 1960. *To Kill a Mockingbird*. New York: Warner Books.

Lee, M. G. 1992. *Finding My Voice*. New York: Bantam Doubleday Dell.

L'Engle, M. 1962. *A Wrinkle in Time*. New York: Dell.

Levine, G. C. 1997. *Ella Enchanted*. New York: HarperCollins.

Lowry, L. 1989. *Number the Stars*. New York: Dell.

Mazer, N. 1997. *When She Was Good*. New York: Arthur A. Levine Books.

Meyer, C. 1993. *White Lilacs*. Orlando, FL: Harcourt Brace.

Namioka, L. 1994. *April and the Dragon Lady*. San Diego: Browndeer Press.

Nixon, J. L. 1993. *The Name of the Game Was Murder*. New York: Dell.

Nolan, H. 1996. *Send Me down a Miracle*. San Diego: Harcourt Brace.

O'Brien, R. C. 1975. *Z for Zachariah*. New York: Atheneum.

Paterson, K. 1991. *Lyddie*. New York: Trumpet Club.

Paulsen, G. 1987. *Hatchet*. New York: Puffin.

———. 1991. *Nightjohn*. New York: Bantam Doubleday Dell.

———. 1991. *The River*. New York: Delacorte.

———. 1997. *Sarny*. New York: Delacorte Press.

Rinaldi, A. 1997. *An Acquaintance with Darkness*. San Diego: Harcourt Brace.

Ruby, L. 1993. *Miriam's Well*. New York: Scholastic.

Rylant, C. 1992. *Missing May.* New York: Dell.

Smith, S. 1997. *Crown Duel.* San Diego: Harcourt Brace.

Staples, S. F. 1989. *Shabanu, Daughter of the Wind.* New York: Knopf.

———. 1993. *Haveli.* New York: Knopf.

Tan, A. 1989. *The Joy Luck Club.* New York: Ivy Books.

Taylor, M. 1976. *Roll of Thunder, Hear My Cry.* New York: Bantam.

———. 1981. *Let the Circle Be Unbroken.* New York: Bantam.

White, R. 1997. *Belle Prater's Boy.* New York: Scholastic.

Woodson, J. 1993. *Between Madison and Palmetto.* New York: Dell.

———. 1994. *I Hadn't Meant to Tell You This.* New York: Delacorte.

———. 1994. *Maizon at Blue Hill.* New York: Dell.

Wrede, P. C. 1989. *Snow White and Rose Red.* New York: Tom Doherty Associates.

Yolen, J. 1990. *The Devil's Arithmetic.* New York: Puffin.

———. 1992. *Briar Rose.* New York: Tom Doherty & Associates.

Zindel, P. 1968. *The Pigman.* New York: Bantam Books.

References

Applebee, A. 1989. *The Teaching of Literature in Programs with Reputations for Excellence in English.* Technical Report 1.1. Albany, NY: Center for the Learning and Teaching of Literature.

Bloom, A. 1988. *The Closing of the American Mind.* New York: Simon and Schuster.

Bushman, J. H., and K. P. Bushman. 1997. *Using Young Adult Literature in the English Classroom.* Upper Saddle River, NJ: Merrill.

Carlson, M. A. 1989. "Guidelines for a Gender-Balanced Curriculum in English, Grades 7–12." *English Journal* 78: 30–33.

Carlson, R., and A. Sherrill. 1988. *Voices of Readers: How We Come to Love Books.* Urbana, IL: National Council of Teachers of English.

Christenbury, L. 1993. *Making the Journey.* Portsmouth, NH: Boynton/Cook Publishers.

Daniels, H. 1994. *Literature Circles: Voice and Choice in the Student-Centered Classroom.* York, ME: Stenhouse.

D'Souza, D. 1991. *Illiberal Education: The Politics of Race and Sex on Campus.* New York: Free Press.

Hayn, J. A., and D. Sherrill. 1997. "Female Protagonists in Young Adult Literature." *The ALAN Review* 24: 43–46.

Hirsch, E. D., Jr. 1988. *Cultural Literacy: What Every American Needs to Know.* New York: Vintage.

Purcell, P., and L. Stewart. 1990. "Dick and Jane in 1989." *Sex Roles* 22, 177–84.

Scott, K., and C. Schau. 1985. "Sex Equity and Sex Bias in Instructional Materials." In *Handbook for Achieving Sex Equity Through Education,* edited by S. Klein. Baltimore: Johns Hopkins University Press.

Spiegel, L. A. 1996. *Females in Adolescent Literature.* Ottawa, KS: The Writing Conference, Inc.

Whaley, L., and L. Dodge. 1993. *Weaving in the Women.* Portsmouth, NH: Boynton/Cook.

PART IV

Looking Beyond the Mainstream

The angers between women will not kill us if we can articulate them with precision, if we listen to the content of what is said with at least as much intensity as we defend ourselves against the manner of saying. When we turn from anger we turn from insight, saying we will accept only the designs already known, deadly and safely familiar. I have tried to learn my anger's usefulness to me as well as its limitations.
—AUDRE LORDE, "Uses of Anger," *Sister Outsider*

8

Striking Out

Girl vs. Girl Culture in an Alternative School

ANNEMARIE OLDFIELD

"The girls' fights are the worst."

"The boys can wait and will take it somewhere else, or if they start or look like they're going to start, you can get between them, and they'll stop."

"They'll keep their wits about them no matter how angry they are."

"But not the girls. It's fast; it's emotional; it's fierce. And it's always about a guy. Always."

I heard these words as I was interviewing for a position at an alternative high school in southern New Mexico. In my eight years of teaching English at this school, I have learned how right my future colleagues were, how right they still are. I've broken up many fights, and expect to continue to do so despite the school's recent addition of a security guard. I've seen people seriously hurt in the minutes it takes for the guard to reach the scene. Girls' fights can be vicious. The girls here fight with their fists as well as with their feet and nails. I once watched a girl grab her opponent by an arm and a leg and swing her head forcefully against a locker before I could stop her. I've seen two girls fight so furiously it took five teachers to break them up.

I teach at a small high school in a small town. When there has been an incident that causes girls to be at odds with one another, faculty members can usually sense that something is in the air. It has to do with the way girls bunch, with their furtive looks, their whispers, and their loud outbursts. It has to do with the defiant stance they take when passing one another in the halls, the looks they call "dogging," the derogatory names they mumble. It has to do with the preening looks of the males who are being fought over. Sometimes there's a hint in the usual Monday morning gossip about where the party was, who attended, who came with whom, and who left with someone already spoken for. On those days, members of the staff must be on the lookout, must share information, and must be ready to act when needed. When teachers sense trouble before it begins, they can take steps to initiate conflict mediation, or a least keep the girls out of one another's and harm's way until a solution can be found. Unfortunately, more often the girls find their own solutions in the streets after school, or in the halls or lunchroom.

What precipitates these violent encounters? Typically, the problem begins with a girl who believes a "player's" lies, then gets the truth about his habits thrown in her face. I've talked to many a girl who was pregnant and whose boyfriend had promised marriage after cheating on her the weekend before. The pregnant girl bides her time until she can fight with the one who "stole her man." The guys promise commitment, but as soon as they are out from under the watchful eye of their girlfriends, they will "date" any girl available. "I'm still young," they'll explain to anyone who questions them. The response of the girls they "date"? "She should keep a tighter leash on her old man if she doesn't want me to be with him."

The same girl, six months later, will be ready to fight the next woman in the boyfriend's line of conquests. I've talked with more than one girl who has contracted a venereal disease from a boy, but who continues to take him back because, in her words, "I don't want my baby to grow up without a daddy." Almost without exception, the girl in these scenarios forgives the guy who treated her disrespectfully, and harbors a lasting grudge against the other woman—usually a girl just like herself, caught in the trap of trying to find a man to boost her self-esteem.

Instead of recognizing one another as allies, girls at my school view one another as potential enemies. On the street and in the classroom, they size each other up based on the threat the other might pose in the fierce competition for men. They are rivals in a daily contest, the prize in which is the successful acquisition of some Prince Charming. Few women ever find their prince because, frankly, few true princes exist in the arena in which my girls compete. A baby face, a "bad ride," and a pocket full of money constitute a prince in some neighborhoods, even though money in the pockets of a man who is uneducated and doesn't work is usually drug money. The girls can't see that these men offer only futures of pain. When their "prince" is sent to jail, they revel in the role of martyr and turn to his family and government checks for support.

Other guys have no money but have the easy charm to boost the self-esteem of girls who have spent their lives wanting more. They talk their way into these girls' lives. They have no plan to work; they plan to rely on the checks their girlfriends receive for the baby—for spending money to buy cigarettes, alcohol, and drugs. In order to keep her man, a girl may give him her baby's money so he does not make good on his threat to find someone who will. Many girls will drop out of school to work or to stay home and keep an eye on a guy's activities during the day. It's a question of honor for these girls to keep their man against all comers, even if he is not someone mainstream society would value as worth keeping.

Although an outside observer might be quick to judge them so, these are not stupid girls. The girls I teach are all individuals, beautiful girls with the potential to become intelligent, beautiful, self-assured women. These are girls I come to know and to love. It breaks my heart to admit that most of them will not come anywhere near fulfilling their potential. Despite what we try to teach them in school, many come to believe that college is not an option for them, and that successful careers and quality relationships are even less so. Those who do believe in the dream often get sidetracked along the way. They become pregnant, or their relationships sour. Some must work at menial, low-paying jobs to support themselves and their children because Prince Charming has vanished or lives two blocks away and remains unemployed rather than pay child support. Some of these girls become pregnant as early as thirteen or fourteen, and spend the adolescence they should have had, caring for children rather than exploring options for their own lives. I have again and again asked myself, "How does this happen?" More recently, I've begun to ask, "How do I prevent this from happening to my own daughter?"

I've come to see these girls' pregnancies and dropping out of school as a result of two underlying propositions. First, these girls have set beliefs about gender roles. They believe that a woman's role is to take care of a man's needs whether or not it is convenient, practical, or enjoyable for her. This belief includes most men at most times. The way these girls are expected to take care of their fathers and brothers extends to their attitudes toward their boyfriends. For some of the girls, a subconscious belief guides their behavior, but it's not a belief they would be able or willing to verbalize. In fact, almost all of these girls would argue against the validity of this proposition. They insist that they "don't put up with that," but their blackened eyes and rounded bellies belie their words. They have sex with men and boys whether they enjoy it or not, and many times whether they agree to it or not, because to say no is to invoke male wrath, and "being a rat" is cause for ostracism. They put up with degrading experiences that cause them to be extremely angry, and then, rather than fight the causes of their degradation, they lash out at one another.

The second proposition, the worse of the two, is that the women who should have been responsible for these girls have not become mentors or positive supporters. Rather, they have maintained, protected, and propagated women's roles as caretakers for men. The behaviors I see in young women who fight, both literally and figuratively, for the attention of men are learned behaviors, behaviors that are accepted in their homes, in their friends' homes, in their neighborhoods, in their churches, and in the streets they roam at night. Their behaviors are modeled after those of the women they know: their mothers, grandmothers, aunts, and sisters, who allow themselves to be treated as servants for the men in their lives and who do not usually know to expect any different. These women stay with men who cheat on them with other women and who abuse them when they speak out in protest. The only safe place for them to release their frustrations is with one another. After all, a woman has a fair chance in a fight with another woman.

While we live in a world where many women have made great strides, there are many others who are unaware of or who have not grasped the opportunities before them. Not only do they believe that their current existence is all there is, they pride themselves on their excellence within their limits, fighting and taking care of their men, and they teach their daughters to do the same. Like African women who perform clitorectomies on their daughters to maintain tradition, these mothers set their daughters up to live in service to men and in contention with other women.

Few girls in my classroom are adequately mothered. One semester I had a girl who came to me directly from the middle school, pregnant at thirteen. I struggled to imagine how this could happen, only to discover that her mother is an active member of the drug culture in our town. She holds a job during the day, but snorts cocaine and smokes "rock" at night. Her daughters are left to themselves to navigate the murky waters of the barrio. Five years after the oldest daughter was pregnant at thirteen, the younger daughter repeated the cycle. Her cousin, a twelve-year-old who dressed in the manner of much older, streetwise girls, told me the news with delight, especially repeating the girls' ages as though there were a family contest among the cousins to see who could get pregnant at the earliest age.

Other mothers want to mother and mentor their daughters to keep them safe, but are unable to do so. Many work long hours to support their families and rarely see their daughters during the day. They hope their daughters won't end up in the same situation they are in, but they feel powerless to change their circumstances, powerless to offer them more.

The answer to changing the way young women view themselves and one another is going to be a long and complicated process because its origins run deep within the mores of our culture. My own daughter has been raised with many educational and cultural opportunities that my students lack. Although on one level she understands the gender system and the problems women face, her adolescent tendency to follow the mores of her peers and the outside culture causes me great concern. Outside influences may be stronger than my words. Elizabeth Debold, Marie Wilson, and Idelisse Malave (1993) write about "the wall" that girls hit as they enter adolescence and consciously realize that life is different for men and women, as do many other researchers who focus on the lives of adolescent girls. As a teacher and a mother I know the wall is there, and I struggle daily with ways to lessen the impact girls feel when they hit it. I often feel I am fighting a losing battle.

And yet we must try. Revolution can be a quiet process, a steady wearing away of the structures that rule women's lives. Revolution in my classroom consists of my consciously striving to make a difference in my girls' lives on three levels.

The first level is exposure. The girls I teach must be exposed to other attitudes, other cultures, and other ways of interacting with the world in which they live. Many of my students have never been out of our small town, have never been exposed to women of confidence and power except those women who used their authority to curb the girls' lives.

The second level is instruction. Exposure to the ways that other cultures operate must occasionally include direct instruction of methods that others use to solve conflict and increase self-esteem. When fighting is the main method of handling conflict in homes and neighborhoods, schools are hard pressed to deal with the student behaviors that result. Suspending or otherwise punishing inappropriate student behavior attacks only a symptom of the problem. Direct instruction in conflict resolution and assertiveness training are necessary to attack the problem.

The third level is protection. Girls must be given a protected environment in which to explore the new ideas they are learning. A girl who sees and hears about the possibilities available for women, but who is a victim of harassment and abuse in the very institution in which she is exposed to those possibilities, is not going to be open to them.

Any teacher can include exposure to other attitudes, even within the most restrictive curriculum. I do not advocate a Women's History Month or a unit on women in literature. Schools don't have Men's History Month or units on men in literature. To include women mainly in segregated units gives students the impression that women are aberrations in history and literature, an impression that plays into the supposition that men are the primary focus of our culture. Instead, women should be an integral part of the curriculum on a regular basis. When teaching biographies, I make sure to include as many biographies of women as I do men, and I am careful to make them about women in as many fields as possible. When teaching summarizing skills, I use articles about women at least as often as I use articles about men. When teaching students to "read" popular films, I ask them to look for specific stereotypes that perpetuate inaccurate messages about women and other minority groups. Women have been active in shaping the world throughout time, but stereotypes of women, rather than historic portrayals, take precedence in the popular culture to which students are exposed. The careful teacher will be sure to include women's roles in history as often as possible within the curriculum, and to expose stereotypes and inequities whenever students encounter them. More important, she will teach students to find and expose the stereotypes themselves.

Like many other conscientious teachers, I am careful to depict women in important roles in our society, exposing students to the accomplishments that women have already achieved and the ensuing possibilities. The girls I teach, however, still don't see accomplishments and possibilities as being available to them. They see few women in their own neighborhoods with the skills necessary to change their lives and to achieve in the wider society. Their most immediate role models are often poor examples of success.

It is important, therefore, to give girls direct instruction in methods for resolving conflict and building self-esteem. I have added a unit for teaching interpersonal relationships in my communication skills classes. My classes are a mix of male and female students, and the information applies to all. We learn about the differences between assertive and aggressive behavior, and about how being totally nonassertive or being too directly aggressive are both harmful to relationships. We learn about the power of words and the need for accurate vocabularies to describe how we feel about what is happening in our lives. We discuss physical aggression and its dangers. We learn about the need to surround ourselves with people who respect us and the need to stay away from people who do not. I've learned to avoid resistance from the males in the class by making sure not to assume that it is only the guys who are directly aggressive and only the girls who are nonassertive. Indeed, that is not always the case.

Not surprisingly, the males are also eager to learn how to smooth the difficulties they encounter in their personal relationships. Teaching students to be able to speak up in appropriate manners about what is bothering them is an important step in resolving conflict at home, at school, and in the neighborhood. It is also an important step in building the self-esteem that girls need in order to believe they can succeed in the ways we teach them are available.

Actively naming problems and instructing students in ways to solve their conflicts is necessary for the third component, creating an environment that protects girls from the abuses prevalent in society, providing them a safe place in which to learn and grow. In my class I have only one rule: Show respect. We all try to abide by that rule. I expect students to show respect for me, for their school environment, for themselves, and for each other. For my students, both girls and guys, respect has been something they earned by being tough enough to make others afraid not to have respect for them. They need to be taught otherwise.

I work hard during the first weeks of class to demonstrate mutual respect as a given component of my classroom environment, no matter what a person's status outside. The quiet, self-effacing girl in the corner will receive the same respect as the "banger" in the other corner. The teacher is the only person in the classroom who can enforce that rule at the beginning, but gradually students will begin to say to one another "Show some respect." Establishing this rule for all in the classroom, and enforcing it fairly, cuts down on the number of improper incidents I need to deal with and gives me time to work on the important task of teaching. On the few occasions when confrontations have escalated in my classroom and I have had no choice but to refer a student to the administration for suspension or expulsion, every student, even the one being sent to the administration, has acknowledged the justice of the decision. They voice the adage, "You do the crime, you do the time." Fortunately, situations in which I must refer students to the administration are rare; our staff is adept at locating potential problems and mediating them.

My students know, however, that showing disrespect for another will cause them trouble in my classroom. I have no tolerance for boys who make harassing comments to girls; nor do I tolerate girls who are proud of their ability to be as tough as the boys and who make harassing comments to them. I watch for it carefully, and I correct it quickly. I correct it in my classroom and in the hallways, in the parking lot and in the local Kmart. Because mutual respect has been established and enforced, correction is not usually considered threatening. Sometimes the correction involves no more than a raised eyebrow that says, "Is that what I taught you?" Sometimes it is a conversation we have at another time and place. Sometimes it is a flat directive: "We do not tolerate that kind of talk here." Most of the time, because of the consistent enforcement of the "show respect" rule, a student's reaction to a correction is a sheepish look and a "Sorry, Miss."

I am careful to write few referrals and to make those I do write count. Were I to write up every instance of harassment, I would be dismissed as a fanatic or a quack by both students and colleagues. I would tend to think of myself as one, too. So, I document, carefully, thoroughly, specifically, if I think there is going to be a problem. "On Monday, Tom said, 'Shut up, you fucking whore,' to Sally." "On Thursday, Tom grabbed his crotch and told Lisa, 'I have something here that will shut your mouth.'" I document if I feel a student is habitually and maliciously misogynistic. Students are repeating learned behaviors. Their friends, and sometimes members of their families, speak this way, and their music choices blast the same words into their vocabularies on a daily basis. These influences certainly do not excuse the behavior, but I treat words used by force of habit differently from words used with malicious intent. Inappropriate word choice by force of habit calls for a less stringent strategy of correction. In many cases, students need only to be reminded or gently reprimanded to help them break bad habits, or at least the practice of them in my classroom.

In the case of Tom, I felt his behaviors necessitated the more stringent approach. Tom continually made lewd comments under his breath to girls in classrooms and hallways. All that we teachers heard were the girls telling him to shut up. Our girls don't rat, but since they were obviously upset, I began to investigate. I asked other teachers who reported the same behaviors. I spoke with a few of the girls who would tell me what Tom had said. Other teachers agreed to begin documenting his behavior, sending referrals when he got out of line. When I looked up from my desk one day to see Tom across the hall gesturing to a girl in the class to come and perform oral sex on him I wrote it up, specifically and using no euphemisms.

Since there was an explicit, documented paper trail by more than one teacher, the principal had no choice but to send Tom home, and plenty of support to defend his decision. Tom was not allowed to return until he entered counseling for his problem. Tom is now back in school, and has not had any repeat offenses. Message sent; message received—not just to Tom but to any of the boys who thought this behavior would be tolerated.

The components I have described as being necessary in the classroom are important—essential—for helping girls. But there is only so much a teacher can do to push against the role-socialization girls are exposed to on a daily basis. There is another level on which women must reach these girls: We must strive to create communities in which girls are exposed to and have access to women who are, in spite of the struggles they still face, functioning, happy adults. When I began thinking about this problem and how to solve it, I decided to talk to some of the girls who appear to be well adjusted and secure. I found that the girls who successfully negotiate adolescence are those who have support systems of other women. The common thread with all of them is that they have been adequately mothered, or supported by other women who knew their struggles and, rather than judging them, provided support. Many of them have had sisters or cousins with whom they were close, or some other sort of a support network that included their mother or other significant female adult. These support systems enabled the girls to retain their dignity and self-esteem in the face of enormous obstacles, and to overcome those obstacles.

I first knew the Garcia girls when I butted heads with the eldest in my English classroom. After an extremely rocky beginning, we grew to respect one another, and our relationship became one in which she could share confidences. We've laughed and cried through her abusive relationship, through her pregnancy, at her graduation, and during her time in beauty school. She is now making a life for herself and her beautiful son. While I don't agree with all of her choices, I am proud of her, and she knows it.

The second sister came to our school a few years later. Because of our staff's relationships with the eldest girl, the second was able to open up to us quickly. Heavily involved with a "baby-face/bad ride/bad money" type of guy, she was able to see her future clearly, and with the support of her mother, her sisters, and women on our staff, she made the painful break. He was soon involved with another girl, who met his demands and became trapped in his expectations. The most studious of the three sisters, the second girl excelled in high school and graduated with honors. She is working in a management position in a local store and plans on attending college soon.

The youngest sister is currently enrolled in our high school. When she first came, she was determined to show us how tough she was, and she clashed with all of her teachers. Our loyalty to her older sisters made us determined to help her be successful, although there were times when we were close to giving up. Once, after she had made an ugly comment to me in my classroom, I began to laugh and said, "Oh, girl, I know your mother and your sisters; you come from good stock. You'll be okay here, so quit pretending otherwise."

Stunned for a moment, she started to laugh. "Oh, Miss," was her only retort. It took time and patience, but she became successful in school and, although she has completed all the classes she could take from me, we make a point of keeping in touch with one another. She is scheduled to graduate this spring.

I mention these girls because they are part of a community of women in their home. Their mother, while dealing with the realities of the barrio on a daily basis, worked her way through school and got a job as a nurse. A grandmother and aunts helped the mother to raise the three girls. Although the girls were all gang members at one time, all three have fought their way out of the gang (literally), and all three have managed to remain out. It was not easy to do so. The three of them fight for one another and protect one another from all comers, male or female. They recently fought against the slow, painful death of their mother from cancer, caring for her and for one another and keeping the family going. They lost that fight, but are proving again to be survivors. They come back to school for support or advice when they need it: a résumé, a letter of recommendation, job advice, or a shoulder to cry on. We are there for them as often as we can be, but most importantly, they are there for one another, and they recognize other women as allies and as a means of support.

I wish I could say that these women have gone on to college to become rocket scientists or international journalists. That has not been the case. But they have completed high school. They are seeking careers. They are not on welfare, and they do not let men push them around. These girls were fortunate to have had a ready-made community at home and a supportive supplementary community at school. They know that they don't have to view other women as enemies. They are breaking the cycle.

In *Mother Daughter Revolution,* Elizabeth Debold, Marie Wilson, and Idelisse Malave write:

> To oppose the status quo, to betray the culture that expects us to raise daughters who hold men at the center of their lives, to confront the myths of perfection, self-sacrifice, and separation that hold sway for mothering a daughter will not be comfortable. . . . A circle of mothers and a community of women are essential to us in testing strategies and behaviors, sorting out feelings, finding confirmation for our authority, and making choices about where and when to act differently. At a societal level, only true solidarity—ever-larger circles of mothers—can claim the power of mothering and begin to build communities where girls' losses are truly unnecessary. (1993, 261)

Such communities cannot be created by high school teachers alone. Communities such as these will, of necessity, have different levels of support and different levels of success. Communities such as these must originate in the hearts of women who work with girls in all aspects of their lives: at home, at work, at school, and in the wider community. Women must be careful not to judge girls who are currently engaged in what our staff likes to refer to euphemistically as "alternative lifestyles," or to give up on them. These girls may be lost, but women who have achieved can provide them with the directions to get back home. Real change can come about through the grass-roots efforts of women who have achieved professionally and who remember how hard it was to do so. Real change will come about when those who are ahead in the climb reach down and lift up those who are coming behind them.

Reference

Debold, E., M. Wilson, and I. Malave. 1993. *Mother Daughter Revolution: From Betrayal to Power.* New York: Addison Wesley.

9

Taking Black Girls Seriously

Addressing Discrimination's Double Bind

LYNN SPRADLIN

Introduction

The portrait of African American female students as loud and hostile has been painted, and it continues to hang in America's schools. The origin of this portrait is a complex one. When considering African American student motivation to achieve academically, John Ogbu (1974) observes that this motivation is sharply curtailed by black students' awareness of the limited opportunities and institutional discrimination present in American society and schooling. This has led to African American student opposition in school, expressed in a variety of coping strategies that range from overt rebellion to attempts to "pass" as members of the dominant culture. Carol Gilligan (1982) points out that female students have also developed their own coping strategies in America's schools, and generally tend to silence themselves in order to achieve. This is particularly true of adolescent girls, who tend to lose voice or speak "in a different voice" as they begin to question their own perspectives and knowledge.

But since neither of these perspectives fully explains "those loud black girls" (Fordham 1993, 3), we turn to Signithia Fordham to bring the two ideologies together. Her analysis explains how the universal definition of "femaleness" in American society, one that exclusively represents white middle-class women, propels African American women to take on qualities that are stereotypically defined as being male. She suggests that the loudness that is often asserted to be a deleteriously masculine characteristic of African American women is a metaphor for their "contrariness, embodying their efforts to resist consuming images of them" (1993, 4). Hence, Fordham reasons that in

115

order to be taken seriously, the only commandment for women—and particularly African American women—in the academy is not to appear as woman.
This chapter explores the status and treatment of African American female
high school students in American society and suggests best practice for breaking the cycle of their suppression in school.

Ogbu's Cultural Ecological Theory: African American Opposition in Schools

According to John Ogbu (1990), two primary forces contribute to the academic success or underachievement of minority students in the United States:

1. the initial terms of their incorporation into American society (be it voluntary or involuntary)

2. the patterns of adaptive responses that different minority groups exhibit
in response to discriminatory treatment they receive from members of the
dominant culture

Ogbu explains that voluntary minorities are immigrants who have come to
the United States seeking greater economic opportunities. These minority
group members tend to believe that hard work and compliance will result in
their ultimate success. Even language barriers seem to gradually give way to
the conforming attitudes and efforts that members of voluntary minority
groups extend.

On the other hand, involuntary minorities are those whose ancestors
were brought to this country against their will and who have suffered slavery
or colonization. These minority group members, such as African Americans,
are denied true assimilation into American society. As a result, African American students, aware that the "system" has historically worked to their disadvantage, often choose not to adopt the compliant behaviors that have typically
led to the academic success of voluntary minority students. Instead, they are
more likely to reject dominant culture paths to success.

Fordham, who conducted extensive ethnographic research in a poor,
urban, predominantly black high school in Washington, D.C., corroborates
Ogbu's theory. She found that within the school structure, black adolescents
consciously and unconsciously sensed that they had to forfeit aspects of their
racial identities in order to achieve in school:

[F]or many of them, the cost of school success was too high; it implies that
cultural integrity must be sacrificed in order to "make it." For many Black
adolescents, that option is unacceptable. For the high achievers . . . achieving school success is marked not only by conflict and ambivalence, but by

the need to camouflage efforts and behaviors that the group identifies as "acting white." (1988, 81–82)

As part of their attempt to gain and maintain integrity in the face of discrimination, many of the African American students turned to "cultural inversion," the dismissal of certain forms of behavior, symbols, and meanings as being inappropriate because they are characteristic of white America:

> The subtle opposition of cultural inversion appears to be a frequent response to conquest and domination. Unable to overtly display their displeasure or opposition to the social structure which limits their obtainment of the most highly valued social goals, those social groups excluded from the cultural center of the social system frequently resort to methods which are considered inappropriate by the conquering group, but which at the same time enable the dominated group to retain some sense of self respect and group identity. (1982, 7)

On Being Seen and Not Heard: Creating Adolescent Female Silence

As members of another kind of underclass in a patriarchal society, females also face pervasive barriers to academic achievement in our educational system. For example, female students more often express the existence of gaps in their learning, and more frequently doubt their intellectual competence, than male students do. Belenky, Clinchy, Goldberger, and Tarule note that:

> For many women, the real and valued lessons learned did not necessarily grow out of their academic work but in their relationships with friends and teachers, life crises, and community involvements. . . . Women often feel alienated in academic settings and experience formal education as either peripheral or irrelevant to their central interests and development. . . . The commonly accepted stereotype of women's thinking as emotional, intuitive, and personalized has contributed to the devaluation of women's minds and contributions, particularly in Western technologically-oriented cultures, which value rationalism and objectivity. (1986, 4–6)

Girls are systematically discouraged from pursuing studies that would enhance their prospects for well-paying jobs, even though the American school classroom is in many ways a feminine domain. Nearly three-quarters of teachers are women. Young female students generally succeed and even outperform young male students in all or some academic areas. Yet, the culture of the school as it is controlled in male-dominated society is, in fact, masculine (Noddings 1992). And even successful females have less confidence in their abilities than males, higher expectations of failure, habits of dependency, negative attribution styles, weakened leadership skills, and more modest occupational aspirations. Girls are less likely, therefore, to reach their potential than boys (Keating 1990).

For girls, adolescence is a time of particular vulnerability, "[a] point where a girl is encouraged to give over or to disregard or devalue what she feels and thinks" (Brown 1991, 83). As Gilligan (1982) points out, the unique social experiences that males and females confront lead to distinct developmental characteristics that, in turn, shape male and female orientations to academic achievement. She has found that it is often fear of the loss of important relationships that causes many females to silence themselves when they are confronted with sexist discrimination practices during schooling. The pervasive powerless silence among female students, accompanied by their attempts to meet societal demands for female attractiveness and sexiness, shapes a subordinate profile that disavows female student academic ability and full appreciation of self (Fine 1993).

Thus, female dependent behaviors that are reinforced in American society become reproduced in schools, where a reward structure of docility is valued. Because females, according to Keating, gain praise for quiet behavior, neat work, and conformity, they also learn to become silent in refraining from exercising assertive behaviors in the classroom that are typically associated with achievement and masculinity:

> Girls have been shown to hide their academic weaknesses and avoid intellectually challenging activity in order to maintain teacher approval. . . . Some research even suggests that the reinforcement of passive behaviors in schools actually diminishes ability, and that declining IQ scores for some students are traceable to indications of shy, passive, dependent approaches to learning. Inasmuch as these attitudes differentiate boys' and girls' behaviors, schools effectively risk decreasing female students' ability by reinforcing acquiescent behavior. (1990, 100)

Female silencing strategies quite logically lead to weaker academic achievement. In order to achieve, female students may, therefore, engage in gender "passing" by acting in more stereotypically masculine ways in order to be accepted and to advance. After studying the academic behaviors of 181 fifth- and sixth-grade, white, middle-class students, Lever concluded that "if a girl does not want to be left dependent on men, she will have to learn to play like a boy" (1976, 10). Fordham (1993) agrees that female students are compelled to pass as male dominant others.

Understanding African American Female Student Success and Opposition to a Marginalized Image

As members of at least two subordinate minority groups in American society, African American female students face a double bind of discrimination. How is it, then, that they generally do better than African American male students in school? The answer lies in the variety of coping strategies that African American students use to address the widespread discrimination they face. White and black women are both sanctioned for characteristically male behavior; therefore, many African American female achievers may choose to silence themselves in order to be accepted, as is often the case for white adolescent females. However, because African American women are commonly seen as being "male-like" in their assertiveness or loudness, black female achievers may choose, instead, to "pass" as white and ultimately white male. So, whereas African American males are most likely to oppose schooling in ways that lead to underachievement, as Ogbu (1992) explained, African American female adolescents are more likely than their black male counterparts to "pass" as white males in order to achieve.

Fordham notes that the "gender passing" coping strategy described here is seldom explored as part of the social context of school culture, nor is it often "identified as a factor producing asymmetrical outcomes in African American males' and African American females' school performance" (1993, 5).

Ironically, because African American females are the more successful students, they also are the most ignored by educators. These students are thus socialized to employ a survival strategy that denies them opportunities for true academic advantage and fulfillment. Their loudness is said to alienate them from their teachers, who may perceive them to be unruly and irreverent. To address this problem, they may try to distance themselves from this image. In so doing, they may not feel connected to their own voices, which may now speak not from the heart but from conditioning. Their school success conceals their need to be truly challenged academically and to engage productively in the curriculum with their teachers.

It is particularly painful and costly for African American female students, whose coping strategies tend to worsen their relations with other groups that may find their adopted behavior pattern displeasing, threatening, and unfamiliar. So, their socialization to "pass" is an inordinate price to pay for academic success, mostly because it leads to "ignorance of connections" (Fordham 1993, 23). African American female students, therefore, typically face a lack of social support and then develop ambivalence or uncertainty about their relationships, academic goals, accomplishments, talents, and futures.

African American Female Status and Implications: Fordham's Analysis

Fordham observes that "White and middle class are hidden transcripts of femaleness, the womanhood invariably and historically celebrated in academe. In striking contrast, Black womanhood is often seen as the antithesis of White women's lives, the slur or the nothingness" (1993, 4). Because white womanhood is the cultural universal, the different experience that black women encounter in American schooling is not acknowledged. This is true even though Fordham notes that the history of African American womanhood greatly differs from that of white and other types of womanhood, including:

1. more than two hundred years in which their status as women was annulled, compelling them to function in ways that made them virtually indistinguishable from their male slave counterparts;

2. systemic absence of protection from African American and all other American men;

3. construction of a new definition of what it means to be female out of the stigma associated with the black experience and the virtue and purity affiliated with white womanhood; and

4. hard work (including slave and domestic labor), perseverance, assertiveness, and self-reliance. (8)

Slave history largely negated gender differences between males and females, leaving the African American female image either gender neutral to occupy an ambiguous role in American society, or associated with promiscuity, since the black female slave was blamed for her own rape by her white master. The image of black woman is sullied by a history in which it has been linked with "sex, dirt, housework, and badness" (Palmer 1989, 138). As such, African American females are not included in the definition of white womanhood that has become synonymous with what it means to be female in American culture. Not represented in the cultural universal, African American females are denied the option of utilizing typically female coping strategies as they negotiate oppression in society and schooling. Instead, they are more likely to create success strategies in school that more accurately address and respond to the unique combination of sex and race discrimination they face.

Fordham's (1988) study at Capital High School found that successful black girls achieved their success by attempting to either become or remain silent, or by impersonating a male image using symbolically male speech patterns, writing style, voice, and thinking. However, Fordham explains the silence of the African American females differently from Gilligan's translation of silencing enacted by white females, seeing it not as acquiescence, but rather as:

> an act of defiance, a refusal on the part of the high-achieving females to consume the image of "nothingness" so essential to the conception of the African-American woman. This intentional silence is also critical in the rejection and deflection of the attendant downward expectations so pervasive among school officials. (10)

While assertive behavior is a more natural response of black women to the combination of race and sex discrimination, many African American female students believe that they cannot afford to use strategies that might alienate those in charge. For them, being taken seriously also means dissociating themselves from the image of "those loud black girls" whose refusal to conform to standards of "good behavior" without actually entering the realm of "bad behavior" by . . . breaking school rules which severely undermines their limited possibilities for academic success. (22)

Sadly, little or no attention is paid to African American female students' social context and experience in America's schools. Yet, these students require special attention from educators who are committed to helping to break the cycle of these girls' lost potential.

Taking Black Girls Seriously: Strategies for Success in Teaching

I suggest a four-pronged approach for addressing the needs of African American female high school students in the classroom. Teachers must:

1. create a space in which African American female students feel comfortable actively engaging in the curriculum;
2. openly and consistently seek out African American female students individually to develop substantive relationships with them one on one;
3. maintain an attitude of interest and belief in African American females' abilities and resources; and
4. develop and utilize effective intercultural communication skills.

Creating a Space for Authenticity

African American students generally recognize attention given to African American history and cultural orientation in schooling. Providing such a component integrated into the curriculum will help send an indication of appreciation and alliance. African American perspectives can be presented in a variety of ways in different subject areas. The key is to be accurate and comprehensive in your understanding of the material, and to present the material from an African American perspective as legitimate knowledge and not anecdotal, adjunct information that is brought into the classroom merely because it is interesting to note.

Making each student responsible for class contributions is another method for creating a space for reluctant, yet significant, student expression. Requiring students to research different (perhaps carefully assigned) topics and report their findings and interpretations to the class is a good way to force them to make a stand and communicate their ideas about important issues within the context of the class.

Another way to ensure that students feel free to raise and discuss issues of importance to them is to allow them to do so anonymously by writing questions or comments on index cards that are read aloud in class and answered. Sometimes students are more able and willing to state their opinions and challenge ideas when they are not identified.

Making the First Move Toward Relationship

Using journals is essential for coaxing hesitant students to genuinely communicate regularly with the instructor. Enough structure must be provided to help students learn to address significant topics in journals and to encourage expression of their strongly held beliefs about important issues. Disclosing the teacher's own feelings and beliefs in students' journals in response, while challenging students to question, models the expectation that the teacher is seeking an authentic and respectful relationship with the student.

Journals also provide a safe space in which teachers can confront their own biases. Upon reading responses from students, teachers can identify personal biases by sharing particularly troubling student statements with a trusted colleague. In this setting, teachers can examine the feelings they associate with the statements in order to search for their own interpretations, conceptions, motivations, and meanings. Educators must acknowledge that personal biases exist and find a systematic method for adequately addressing them. In this way, teachers do not allow their biases to interfere with their instruction, which would serve to further discriminate against the students.

Holding individual, private conferences on a regular basis with all students offers teachers opportunities to join in a meaningful manner with students. Making conferences a time to explore ideas and to share feelings about issues and class dynamics leads to relating rather than evaluating. Teachers commonly use individual conferences to scold students individually and to judge students' work privately. Instead, conferences can be used as a time to share with students what they are doing well and what the teacher has noticed about their classroom interaction, and to share the teacher's own personal insights and experiences. Conference time should be used to direct a girl's attention to areas that will benefit her as a student.

Walking the Talk

Finding out as much as one can about the accomplishments, history, culture, perspectives, issues, and resources of African American women is a definite starting place for creating positive attitudes about African American female students. Discussing newfound knowledge with the class in an organized manner that is rooted in the curriculum will model effective growth strategies and validate the importance of the information. It is also helpful to talk to students about why the material is important to the teacher. Such a strategy will illustrate appreciation for and interest in the subject matter. Through it all, a strongly voiced knowledge that African American women can and do succeed in a variety of fields is essential. African American female students must hear that their teachers are advocates and allies in order to feel comfortable joining with them as active participants in their own education.

African American students must also hear their teachers praising them for their original thoughts. Teachers often formulate convergent questions to each of which there is only one correct answer. When students are asked divergent questions, instead, each of which may be answered in a number of ways, discussion is facilitated and students are rewarded for their input that does not necessarily conform to the perspectives presented by the instructor. Teachers must find ways to express approval for original thought and student innovation. Finding ways to provide positive feedback, recognition, and reward to students for their inventions will result in accelerating their academic curiosity, their growth, and their trust in their educational relationship with their teachers. The educator thus demonstrates for these students a substantial payoff for hard work that they do not often perceive.

Developing a network of persons who are willing to mentor African American female high school students is an excellent way to acknowledge and extend these students' educational resources. Providing expectations and training for mentors is a necessity. I use a group mentoring approach in order to maximize the available community resources. Specifically, three to five mentors meet weekly with five to seven students to discuss school climate issues, community resources, African American history and current treatment in

American society, gender differences, and expectations. My goal is to equip the mentors with topics that provide a flexible structure within which they are better able to help their group of students grapple with academic, social, and political forces that affect their achievement and future success. This arrangement also serves to decrease the tendency for students to become dependent on their mentors. Because mentors are often not able, due to time constraints, to serve as mentors in the true sense of the word, this arrangement allows them to be available to the students without taking up an unreasonable amount of their time. Students see that the mentors' role is to help them generate ideas, allocate resources, and provide information. As such, students are less likely to expect mentors to serve as their personal advisors or as "fix-it" persons for their personal and academic problems.

Students are asked to come prepared each week with questions for the group of mentors. In taking on this responsibility, they come to understand that they may direct the focus of the discussion to meet their own individual needs when necessary. However, because mentors take responsibility for presenting information on predetermined topics, students are provided with a structure that enhances their personal and academic growth, and helps them meet the goals they formulate at the beginning of the mentoring relationship, by addressing specific areas of focus. I provide a comfortable and consistent space for group mentoring meetings, complete with refreshments, removing this responsibility from the mentors. I prefer that mentors use their time for talking with students rather than arranging for meals and meeting spaces. In addition, I provide each participant with a copy of two books that they may discuss at each meeting.

The group of mentors and the group of students are each asked to agree on one book that they would like to have the other group read. Once the book choices are made, I purchase copies for everyone. The group mentoring sessions then begin to take on the feel of a book club at several of the weekly meetings. Mentors and students take turns facilitating the book chapter discussion in pairs. This rotation of responsibility is another way to help students see that they are a critical element in the process. This component of the program is empowering for the students because it encourages them to see themselves as having insight and opinions to contribute.

I show my enthusiasm for the program in very concrete, as well as attitudinal, ways. By providing the space, refreshments, and books, I back up my commitment to the mentors and students with money. I attend sessions when invited and present myself as another resource that can be tapped by the students. All three parties, mentors, students, and I (the program organizer), thus demonstrate a vested interest in the success of the endeavor. This aspect is crucial. All parties must feel equally valued and respected as their contributions are expected and built upon throughout the process of the semester-long program.

The success of the program is measured through evaluations conducted at the end of the semester. Mentors, students, and I describe the benefits and deficiencies of the program offerings. In addition, I compare students' absenteeism and grades during the program to those before the program. Typically, students state feelings of great satisfaction with the program and list many personal gains. Students' GPAs tend to remain the same or increase, while their absentee rates remain the same or decrease, following their participation in the program. My sense is that students benefit from the group support that they would not have in a one-to-one mentoring situation, and leave the program feeling like they are part of a group—and that the group is a force that can be harnessed to meet their complex layers of needs.

Demonstrating Intercultural Competence

Most African American female students are taught by white teachers, or by black teachers who may be perceived to be "sell-outs" by African American female students. Because of this, intercultural competence is a knowledge and skill area that must be explored. Enrolling in group counseling or a discussion group (like a book club) with a diverse membership will give teachers practice sharing the leadership role in discussion and giving and receiving effective feedback during group interaction. Teachers must learn to function as facilitators rather than as evaluators during class discussions, although this change in role function is not an easy one to make. It is important that teachers learn and then model respectful and effective ways to offer support and to confront students' views as valuable aspects of the group process. Teachers must help students understand what group process is, how it works, and what the expectations are for each participant.

Whenever the subject of diversity enters into the typical classroom discussion, the potential for resistance occurs. Displaying hostility, withdrawing from participation, dominating class time through questioning, invalidating the content or the instructor, and other distancing stances are common among all students. Being well prepared to deal with such behavior is crucial. Teachers should practice beforehand by discussing material with colleagues, friends, and family in intercultural group settings, taking note of sources of strong reaction and disagreement and asking for questions and feedback from the practice audience participants. Educators cannot ignore this aspect of effective communication when preparing to teach diverse groups of students.

Teachers must be prepared to accept students' expression of disagreement and conflict as previously unexamined perspectives are explored and presented from a variety of discussion participants.

Conclusion

Preparing to teach African American female high school students is not without pain, difficulty, and uncertainty on the part of the teacher. It must include a review of relevant historical information, an understanding of African American female perspectives, opportunities to interact with African American women, the transformation of various negative stereotypes about African American women, and the development of effective intercultural communication skills. Through this process, the work necessary for breaking the cycle of suppression of African American female students can begin. Teachers must help students make connections and learn to profit from their investigations and ingenuity.

The most important question an educator should keep in mind when preparing to teach these students is multifaceted: What do I want these students to know about themselves, their world, their classroom, and their teacher? Once this question is addressed within a culturally inclusive context, the implementation of effective teaching strategies is imminent.

References

Belenky, M., B. Clinchy, N. Goldberger, and J. Tarule. 1986. *Women's Ways of Knowing*. New York: Basic Books.

Brown, L. 1991. "Telling a Girl's Life: Self-Authorization as a Form of Resistance." In *Women, Girls, and Psychotherapy: Reframing Resistance*, ed. C. Gilligan, A. Rogers, and D. Tolman, 71–86. New York: Harrington Park Press.

Cook, E. 1993. *Women, Relationships, and Power: Implications for Counseling*. Alexandria, VA: American Counseling Association.

Fine, M. 1993. "Sexuality, Schooling, and Adolescent Females: The Missing Discourse of Desire." In *Beyond Silenced Voices: Class, Race, and Gender in United States Schools*, ed. L. Weis and M. Fine, 75–100. Albany: State University of New York Press.

Fordham, S. 1982. "Cultural Inversion and Black Children's School Performance." Paper presented at the annual meeting of the American Anthropological Association, December. Washington, DC.

————. 1988. "Racelessness as a Factor in Black Students' School Success: Pragmatic Strategy or Pyrrhic Victory?" *Harvard Educational Review* 58: 54–84.

————. 1993. "Those Loud Black Girls: (Black) Women, Silence, and Gender 'Passing' in the Academy." *Anthropology and Education Quarterly* 24: 3–32.

Gilligan, C. 1982. *In a Different Voice: Psychological Theory and Women's Development.* Cambridge, MA: Harvard University Press.

Keating, P. 1990. "Striving for Sex Equity in Schools." In *Access to Knowledge,* ed. J. Goodlad and P. Keating, 91–106. New York: College Board Publications.

Lever, J. 1976. "Sex Differences in the Games Children Play." *Social Problems* 23: 478–87.

Noddings, N. 1992. "The Gender Issue." *Education Leadership,* 65–70.

Ogbu, J. 1974. *The Next Generation: An Ethnography of Education in an Urban Neighborhood.* New York: Academic Press.

————. 1990. "Minority Education in Comparative Perspective." *Journal of Negro Education* 59: 45–55.

————. 1992. "Understanding Cultural Diversity and Learning." *Educational Researcher* 21:5–24.

————. 1993. "Difference in Cultural Frame of Reference." *International Journal of Behavioral Development* 16: 483–506.

Palmer, P. 1989. *Domesticity and Dirt: Housewives and Domestic Servants in the United States.* Philadelphia: Temple University Press.

PART V

Out-of-School Literacy Commitment

Entry into junior high presents a critical juncture of . . . necessary un-learning and relearning. Adults and adolescents must all renegotiate their roles and relationships—roles and relationships informed not simply by entry into adolescence but also by how adolescence is socially situated within multiple cultural, historical, and institutional settings.

—MARGARET J. FINDERS, *Just Girls*

10

Who's at Risk? Entering the World of Adolescent Zines

ELIZABETH DUTRO, JENNIFER SINOR,

AND SARA RUBINOW

Amanda is in the tenth grade and is writer, editor, and publisher of her own zine. Each issue is filled with politically charged art, poetry, fiction, and reflections, and is sent out to dozens of other young authors ("zinesters") who share her passion for writing in this genre. Armed with paper, glue stick, and scissors, Amanda creates collages of words and pictures, often choosing to ignore conventions of grammar and spelling. The stories and commentaries she writes celebrate her feminist politics, and reveal how those politics work to alienate her from her school peers. At many suburban middle and high schools, girls like Amanda are busy writing and designing elaborate publications, transforming their local Kinko's into their own personal publishing houses. It is these zines, their authors, and the implications this phenomenon holds for classrooms that we explore in this chapter.

In his book *Zines and the Politics of Alternative Culture*, Stephen Duncombe defines zines as "noncommercial, nonprofessional, small circulation magazines which their creators produce, publish, and distribute by themselves" (1997, 6). He describes them as part of an "underground world" that exists apart from and continually critiques the mainstream culture; they are spaces in which authors work out their identities in relation to that culture. Although there are many kinds of zines, including fanzines and adult women's zines, we are interested in zines written by adolescent girls. Primarily middle-class and female, adolescent zinesters draw on multiple genres to explore one primary theme: themselves and the political and social world that surrounds them. Most zines are autobiographical, unveiling in words and images a portrait of an adolescent life. Like most zinesters, those in our study are primarily white, middle-class girls. Two of the participants are Asian American. All of the zinesters live in suburban communities and range in age from thirteen to nineteen.

We are interested in zines as both an unofficial literacy practice and as a form of autobiography practiced by adolescent writers. We brought to our research a particular interest in the ways in which young writers work through identity issues—specifically around gender—in their zines. We also explored zine writing as a social phenomenon, creating and sustaining a community of zinesters that transcends geographic borders. Our readings of zines and conversations with zinesters suggest that most zinesters view themselves as outside of the mainstream of adolescent life. The majority of zines we read are explicitly political, and it is, in part, these politics by which zinesters locate themselves outside of the mainstream. All of the zinesters in our study identified with the political left and were often explicit in their feminist agendas, their criticism of homophobia and racism, and their explorations of how gender operates in their lives. It seems to us that the zine community is built and sustained largely through the zinesters' need to connect with others who share their political convictions. We examined both the process and product of zine writing through interviews with zinesters, their responses to a questionnaire, and close readings of several zines.

Feminist literary critic Sidonie Smith writes, "If we are not telling our stories, we are consuming other people's lives" (Smith and Watson 1996, 3). In trying to show the fact that we are consuming the zinesters' stories, we feel it is important to engage in that same risky practice of autobiographical writing. Therefore, we tell a few of our own stories alongside those of the zinesters. In addition to sharing in the risk of personal writing, we use our stories to explore the conflicts we felt in researching the underground world of zines.

As former teachers and as researchers who work with young people, we have witnessed the many ways that students take the official literacy practices we teach them and transform them into acts of creativity that we could not have imagined. This has been our experience with zines. We feel fortunate and privileged that the zine community has been open and willing to share its art and passion with us. We believe that educators can learn valuable lessons from listening to the zinesters' voices, lessons that can positively affect the literacy learning of young people. As Shirley Brice Heath reminds us, "learners frequently display in out-of-school contexts skills relevant to using literacy which are not effectively exploited in school learning environments" (1994, 54). At the same time, however, we realize that there are implications for our treading into this underground world. In Smith's terms, we are consuming the lives of these young authors, and we must examine the implications of appropriating their voices and lives for use in research as well as classrooms.

The Zinesters

Sara: *Although I had published my own "underground" magazine in high school, I wasn't aware of zines until my college years when the "riot grrrl" movement was peaking in visibility. Later, when I was student teaching, I discovered that one of my students, Anthony, had just printed up his first zine, which he wrote with his girlfriend, Chris. We began talking about zines, and as our conversations grew, I began to envision a research project. Anthony and Chris supported this idea and introduced me to their zine community. In their zine, they wrote: "Sara . . . is doing a really neat project pertaining to zines and who does them and why. Just tell her why you do yr zine or why people do zines. Yr voice counts! So please write her back if she requests a copy of yr zine & letter. Thank you." Anthony and Chris validated my voice, a voice that none of the other zinesters had heard. Our conversations made their way to the pages of their next issue as well, when Anthony wrote: "I first started thinking about the value of zines with Sara, the student teacher we had in American Literature. . . . To Sara zines are important because they allow kids to do something creative and important and still be kids with spelling errors and angst trips. She believes zines serve to give kids a community to interact and grow with." Zines are about the exchange of ideas, the validation of voice, and the creation of community. Though I'd never published a zine, I was woven into the zine community. I was appreciative of my position, but also wary. I was not a zinester, but not an outsider either. This position informs my research. I approach zines as a researcher, looking through the lenses of different theories, arriving at conclusions, and thinking about educational practice. As I do this, I'm ever mindful of the fact that the zinesters have privileged me with their stories. And as I take their stories to new places and new audiences, I feel I must keep the zinesters informed about the directions our research is taking, how audiences are reacting, and what the next step might be. I care about their reactions. Without them, I have nothing to say, nothing to write. They are the story.*

The popularity of personal zines rose as a result of the "riot grrrl" movement, which is defined, in part, through political beliefs that are also reflected in the zines. That movement, one with which many of the zinesters in our study closely identify, is explicitly antisexist, antiracist, antihomophobic, and pro-girl. Part of the movement's purpose is to create a space for girls who share these political beliefs and who often feel alienated—in part because of those beliefs—from their schools and communities. Zines are one way in which girls carve out that space, a space in which an alternative community of like-minded peers communicate with and support each other. We contacted members of that community and asked zinesters to fill out a questionnaire in which they reflect on their decision to publish zines and what motivates them to continue.

Many of the girls' responses indicate that the zine community grows from a need for connection and validation. The zinesters speak of their desire to communicate their thoughts and beliefs through writing. They consistently speak of the importance of connecting with peers who share their worldview. As Tara writes, "I was suicidal, anorexic, and feeling alienated in a suburban school system. [Writing zines] was a way of expressing myself and networking with the like-minded. My life took a turn for the better. . . . I think it was the introduction of zines, not Prozac, that literally saved my life." Although Tara's experience with zines is particularly dramatic, others echo her relief at finding a method for making meaningful connections with peers. Krista writes, "I had nothing to do and really nobody to communicate with in my town at the time. . . . [Writing zines] was a way to be intellectually and emotionally validated by a like-minded group of people." Other girls also write of "getting my work out to other people . . . that were doing the same thing, who had a connection to me." At a time in their lives when validation and acceptance from peers is extremely important, these girls express feelings of alienation and disconnection from their schools and geographic communities. It is with a sense of relief that they describe their discovery of zines and their—often newfound—feelings of belonging and connection.

Zinesters maintain their community by providing feedback to each other, often within the pages of the zines in the form of cross-references to other girls' zines and reviews of other zines. Zinesters will also give feedback to one another in the form of personal notes and letters. This feedback was very important to the girls who responded to our questionnaire, for it provided tangible evidence of their place in the zine community. One zinester reports that feedback is the proof that "I'm not alone." As Sierra writes, "If it wasn't for a few people who write to me and tell me that something I said struck them or mattered to them or made them think, I could not do this anymore. Feedback is basically the only thing that matters to me at this point." Like her zinester sisters, Sierra risks her deepest held beliefs and details of her everyday life in the pages of her zine, and it is crucial that she feel that she is not speaking into a vacuum. Similarly, Tara describes feedback as the "fuel that I live on. Even if I offend someone, I'm glad that I made them THINK about what they feel and why they think it." These zinesters are motivated to continue writing and publishing when they know that their writing affects their readers. The feedback makes the writing worth the risk.

In return for a copy of their zine, most writers request a dollar and postage to cover the cost of photocopying and mailing. They will also accept a zine in exchange for their own. Unlike mainstream publications, zines are never meant to be profit-making enterprises. The reward is in the interaction with and connection to the audience. This audience is not abstract, made up of readers unknown to the author; rather, the audience and the zinester interact continually. This reciprocity is why many zinesters refer to their fellow authors as "pen pals." The zinesters' writerly identity is formed, in part, through her relationship with her audience. As one girl tells her readers, "Without you all it just wouldn't be possible." Her audience is the impetus for all of those hours she spends standing at the photocopier at Kinko's, and hunched over her kitchen table with scissors, paper, and a glue stick. Yet, that intimate relationship with the audience imbues an element of self-consciousness into zinesters' writing. As self-conscious writers connecting to a particular audience, they are each actively constructing a self on the page, a self that is defined by both what they choose to reveal and what they choose to keep to themselves. As Grace says, "People only really know what you tell them."

This conscious construction of self is a complicated issue for many zinesters because, as one girl put it, "The whole idea of zines [is supposed to be] pure, unbridled thoughts, rants, poems, art, lists, prose, reviews . . . purely that person." Some zinesters told us that they have trouble reconciling that ideal with the reality of writing. One made the insightful comment that "If I were to reconcile the 'real me' and the 'zine me,' I'd have to start a new zine!" Sierra says, "I censor myself because there are so many nuances of my day-to-day life that affect me, but wouldn't matter to anyone not in my immediate vicinity." Another girl states, "I am aware of what I do and don't feel comfortable saying and printing."

Other girls believe that the self-portraits they present in their zines are not personas, but represent their "true" selves. One zinester says, "I'm not different than my zine. I do whatever I want to. That's what's so beautiful about zines." Another agrees, claiming that "The me in my zine is as close to the me in real life as you can convey through writing and a photocopier." Whether or not the individual zinester feels that she is actively constructing herself, she clearly writes for an audience and is, therefore, conscious of the fact that her words will be read and that she will be interpreted through them. As one zinester says, "Sometimes I censor bits of my life, but I try not to—I do try to leave out depressing factors that I don't see as benefiting the audience."

This awareness of audience, expressed so clearly in their responses to the questionnaire, is also sometimes apparent in their zines. For example, one zinester introduces a topic by writing, "I feel a bit weird writing about this because I don't want it to be seen as too self-effacing or as some cry for compliments or whatever, but it is something I think about a lot." Another finishes a page by saying, "I just think I'm lucky to have the opportunity to watch myself grow and change not only as a writer, but as a person. I'll shut up now. Sorry if that sounded arrogant." For many zinesters, the zine appears to function as a filtered diary, written for an audience beyond the self. They explore intimate details of their lives, yet they control the pen, constructing those details in particular ways and creating a particular persona on the page. It is to the actual pages of the zines that we now turn.

The Zines

Elizabeth: *I pick up a zine to read and feel like an intruder initially. I remind myself that I'm an invited guest in this community and then I feel less an intruder and more like Charlie, grasping the golden ticket that privileges him to enter the fascinating, alternative world that exists behind the gates of Willy Wonka's chocolate factory. I'm being allowed to eavesdrop and share what I overhear with other adults. I want to tread carefully here, avoid arrogance, respect the rights and property of my gracious hosts (I want to be Charlie, the honest guest, not the children whose greed leads them to become blueberries or to wallow in lakes of liquid chocolate). Reading the zines, I feel privy to the intimate conversations of close friends, conversations like those I had with my closest friend when I was in high school. She and I would sit talking on my bed, late at night, afghans wrapped around our pajama-clad bodies, busily critiquing our classmates. Those girls didn't acknowledge our presence in school, and it was important for us to talk about their shortcomings, the things about which they were ignorant and we were knowledgeable. Through those talks, we explored our fledgling feminism and vented about our positions in the social hierarchies of school. Would I have wanted the contents of those talks revealed to my schoolmates? Of course not. My words were meant only for the trusted ears of my best friend and I, in turn, closely guarded her confidences. The zine community is certainly more public than my midnight conversations, but its writings have the feel of confidences shared with close friends, friends who wouldn't dream of betraying you, exposing you to the harsh criticism of outsiders. I am the supposed benign outsider, one who can be trusted. I'm not looking to be rewarded for my honesty; I don't need a ride in the glass elevator. I just want the factory to be running as smoothly when I leave as it was when I arrived.*

The zines we have read are filled with girls' stories of confronting or overcoming sexism and homophobia. They are also filled with the feelings of ridicule they suffer when they identify themselves as feminists. The girls assert their feminism with pride in the zines, yet between the lines lies a degree of very real pain inflicted by the cruel words and tauntings of unsympathetic peers. The feminist identities that these girls can assert so proudly in their zines take real courage and resilience to announce in their everyday lives. As the girls expressed in their survey responses, it is with relief that they take their pen and glue stick in hand and connect with peers who share their convictions. Below, we share just a few examples of the many ways that girls explore issues of gender and feminism in their zines.

One consistent theme in Amanda's zine is ambiguous sexual identity. Without dealing explicitly with issues of sexual preference, she writes about her attraction to both males and females. For example, she includes a page devoted to two of her favorite movie actors, Claire Danes and Leonardo DiCaprio. The page includes large pictures of both actors' faces and beside them, in her own printing, Amanda writes, "God, Claire Danes is so cute. So is Leonardo DiCaprio . . . how could you choose one?"

In another issue she showcases the actress who plays Alex Mack on the Nickelodeon television show of the same name: "The girl who plays Alex . . . is super duper cute so that's why she's the centerfold for this issue. . . . I love you alex. The coolest episode of Alex Mack was when she became friends with this total punk rock girl named Lindsay. And alex did her hair purple and put it up in these little buns that looked so rad. I was hoping she and lindsay would get it on but of course it didn't happen. Oh, well." In these examples, Amanda creates an ambiguous sexual identity by writing about her attraction to both male and female actors and her desire to see a homosexual relationship. Yet other times Amanda writes of her interest in boys. For example, she writes that one male school friend is "reel cute." Whether or not Amanda is or ever will be bisexual, her writing, her conscious creation of an ambiguous sexual identity, serves to highlight her gay-positive politics.

Another zinester, Kate, has written a list entitled "Hey Idiot! I thought I might take the time to explain some things that should be obvious." Two items on the list read: "Just because I don't shave my legs and wear men's work clothes doesn't make me a dyke. Just because I paint my nails and can be feminine doesn't make me straight." Like Amanda, Kate chooses not to reveal her sexual orientation to her readers. By remaining sexually ambiguous she is able to emphasize her belief that both homosexuality and heterosexuality are perfectly acceptable, and that her sexual orientation cannot be assumed based on stereotypes of feminine and masculine dress or behavior.

Some of the zinesters do identify themselves as lesbians, which often locates them on the margins of their school communities. One young woman writes that one of her best accomplishments for the year was "Coming 'out.' Surviving and using my struggle to my advantage." Another girl, who does not identify herself as either gay or straight, writes of being called a lesbian by a classmate:

> Kristy . . . once told me, "You know what you're going to be when you grow up?"
>
> "What," I asked, innocently thinking she was gonna tell me what occupation I would be best for—teacher? doctor?
>
> "A lesbian," she answered with a smirk, as if she'd said something really witty, funny, and intelligent.
>
> "What the fuck?" I said. Damn . . . being a lesbian isn't an occupation! Sheesh, and all because I said I was a feminist.

For both girls, sexual identity—proclaimed or assumed—marginalized them in their school communities, a marginalization that they could safely reveal in the pages of their zines. Here they could share their gay-positive politics and critique and condemn the perceived conservative, intolerant views of their school peers.

The girls often use zines to assert their own identities as feminists and to critique their schoolmates—whom they believe are largely clueless about feminism. In a zine yearbook that includes profiles of and writing by zinesters, several of the essays describe the writers' frustrations with their peers' ignorance about feminism and the ways in which the zinesters' identities as feminists work to marginalize them.

Maya writes, "I don't know about y'alls' peers, but at my [Christian] school, people seem to view being a feminist as being wrong (they are all VERY close-minded!)." She goes on to relate specific incidents of sexism at her school and her attempts to explain feminism to other girls in her class: "A gal asked if I was a feminist. 'Yes,' I replied, 'but feminism is basically thinking Women should be equal with men.' She didn't seem impressed."

Amanda starts her essay "I think most of the girls at my school would definitely stand up for themselves if a boy confronted them with a sexist remark. However, there's still a lot of internalized sexism at my school that most people don't notice." Another girl notes that one of the top ten things she hates about school is "kids pointing and laughing at my unshaved legs."

For these girls, part of being a feminist is choosing not to conform to some of the traditional norms of femininity. Their nonconformity is marked through both their style choices (for instance, not shaving) and expressions of personal beliefs and opinions. The politics that make them targets of cruel teasing by their school peers, teasing that must be a source of true hardship in their everyday lives, become something they can celebrate with pride in their zines.

Those politics also include the awareness that girls' voices are not always heard in mainstream culture. Frustration with gender inequity is a primary focus of much of the writing in the zines we read. For example, one zinester writes about her "favorite double standard of all time: men can scratch themselves all they want, but if a woman touches her breasts people think she's disgusting." She recognizes that girls are not allowed the same privileges as boys, and that similar behavior does not ensure similar response. In this example and in many discussions of everyday things, such as bras and tampons, and of icons of pop culture, such as Pamela Anderson Lee, each zine reflects the girls' awareness of and discontentment with their position in society.

One zinester writes about gender inequity in the English classroom: "We were reading *The Awakening* in English and Paul said, 'I don't see why we have to read a girly book!' Boy, did us girls get down on him for that though . . . we kindly pointed out that EVERY OTHER BOOK we'd read that year was written by a man." This girl clearly recognizes the gender imbalance in her school's English curriculum, as well as the arrogance of her male classmate's comment. She relates this story in her zine, confident that the girls in the zine community will share her awareness of the dearth of women writers in the high school English classroom and appreciate her response to Paul.

Through zines, girls can connect with other young feminists and enjoy membership in a community that does not locate them on the margins. This community becomes one place where these girls feel they fit in, where their feminist beliefs are in the mainstream, and where their stories are heard and valued. As we have suggested, it is their security in knowing the identity of their audience and what their audience values that allows these girls to take risks in the ways that they do.

Research and Zines

Research requires telling other's stories. Even in the most quantitative of studies, there are human lives being narrated in the numbers and graphs. It is the responsibility of the researcher to consider her relative position of power and to take into consideration the ways in which her position and her gaze intersect with and affect her interpretations of the stories of those she is studying. Such reflexivity and caution produce research that rests more evenly between subject and object, but it does not guarantee that the effect of the researcher's gaze will not do violence to the subject—especially when, like zinesters, they already occupy marginalized or silenced positions.

Jennifer: *Two years ago I began the project of rereading a text in order to reclaim the voice of a character who was literally silenced. The novel was* Wide

Sargasso Sea *by Jean Rhys—a book in which Rhys attempts to "give voice" to the madwoman in the attic from Charlotte Brontë's novel* Jane Eyre. *And while Rhys does indeed give form and life to Bertha, in the process she creates another silenced character—Bertha's Afro-Caribbean servant, Christophine. My goal was to find Christophine's voice by reading her silences and absences. I approached this project using the same methodological frame that we used in the zines study. I used a feminist approach based on the assumption that structural forces in our society effectively silence or disregard certain groups of people (like adolescent girls and colonized maidservants), and that dismantling these structures, or at least acknowledging their existence, requires that we read and see in new ways. So I did. And at the end of my rereading, Christophine is not only no longer silenced, she is screaming.*

When I completed this project last spring, I presented the results. I thought that I had done a relatively good job of recovering Christophine's voice, and most of those gathered indicated their agreement. And then Susan, an African American professor of psychology, spoke. She charged me with misusing my white, feminist position of privilege to read in ways that suited my own values. What I remember from that conversation is her anger, her aggressiveness, her fast-held belief that I was wrong, and my own inability to respond to her charges because what she said seemed true to me at the time. In effect, Susan told me I had no right to recover this story, even if my intentions were "right." Because I shared little context with Christophine—there were obvious differences in race, class, and life experiences—I could not approach this "other" no matter how reflexive or careful I was. Susan demanded that I be someone I can never be (at the very least, a woman who is not white), or else leave Christophine's story for someone else to tell.

I believed that I had betrayed my subject.

Could a project like this ever succeed? What could be done differently? Or, as Linda Alcoff (1995) asks, is every act of speaking about *an automatic act of speaking* for? *Is there any way, for example, that a white Western woman could ever hear the stories Christophine is telling in her silences, or will she never be able to understand her experience? Is there any way that researchers can read the work of zinesters in ways that do not work to silence them further? Or do the differences in power and position mean that researchers will always reaffirm the positions they are attempting to dismantle?*

This is what is at stake when we conduct research—especially when those we are studying hold marginalized, silenced positions. In our work with zines, we have tried to illustrate the struggles and limitations of our study, and the ways that the publication of this book chapter puts our subjects at a level of risk previously unfelt—one that goes far beyond the calculated risk the zinsters knowingly undertook in sending their zines to each other. By telling our own stories along with theirs, by considering the ways in which we both share in the zinesters' context and remain outside it, and by being reflective in our readings, we hope to have lessened the effect of our gaze, the chance for harm.

We also share with these young women the experience of our adolescences, which were spent in a patriarchal world, as well as our positions as feminists on the political left. In many ways, we live along the margins with them. Such commonality no longer applies to classroom audiences composed of students who have not come together for political, supportive, or creative reasons. This change in audience (and the resulting changes in the reception of zines) is why we turn now to the difficulty of importing zines into the classroom.

Zines and the Classroom

Elizabeth: *With Jennifer and Sara, I was presenting a symposium on zines at a major academic conference. Our session was one of the last on the final day of the conference, and all day we joked about how we would read our papers to each other and a room full of empty chairs. Then, those chairs that I'd imagined vacant begin to fill, and soon we found ourselves speaking to an audience of more than twenty teachers and researchers of English, all listening intently to our stories of zines and zinesters. When we finished, I invited the audience to begin a discussion. A young high school teacher spoke animatedly about the potential of zines for motivating students to write creatively. "You could take the zines," she said, "and spread them on a table for kids to examine. Maybe if they were exposed to this writing, they would want to write similarly." A few other teachers nodded. I knew that zines were something new and different, just the kind of tool that innovative teachers sought to enrich their curricula. Yet I felt my anxiety build, felt the urge to speak. "Hmmm," I began, "I think we have to be careful. The zinesters write for each other; they write for a sympathetic audience. Placing them on a table to be consumed by classrooms of other adolescents potentially exposes them to the same ridicule and marginalization that they are writing to escape." Sara and Jennifer voiced similar concerns. Members of the audience moved on to other points of discussion, and soon our session was over. Many stayed after to talk with us further. This was nice. I felt validated, proud. I also felt successful in complicating the issues surrounding zines, especially the risks inherent in bringing them wholesale into the classroom. Then three teachers in a row asked me where they might find mailing lists to send away for zines; you see, they wanted to collect some for their classrooms. Oh . . . I see.*

As teachers, it is difficult to read about zinesters' commitment to everyday autobiographical acts and not immediately want to import this form of writing into the classroom. These are examples of students engaging in a kind of powerful self-expression not often achieved within the time constraints of a semester or the institutional constraints of public education. There is a great temptation to see zines as an answer to the call of pedagogies that emphasize experience and the students' subject positions. Yet, as we have suggested, one of the reasons zinesters can express themselves in charged and dramatic ways is because they are writing for a specific audience of like-minded zinesters, an audience unlike the one reading this book. As much as we would like to think of ourselves as creators of nontraditional learning spaces in the classroom, we are still very much a part of the institutional forces that zinesters are resisting. And not only are we a part of these institutional forces, we are the ones in relative positions of power.

What would it mean to import zines into the classroom, thus consuming and circulating stories that were not intended for us? To do so—by making zines available for students to read, assigning zines as a project, or asking zinesters to talk about their writing—would be to remove zines from the context in which they were written and the audience for which they were intended. If we accept the premise that for stories to intersect there must first be a shared context, then decontextualizing zinesters' stories and giving them to an audience composed potentially of readers that the authors themselves write against, works to doubly silence those we are trying to empower. We need only to look at the ways in which these young girls talk about the daily abuse, violence, and teasing they receive from their peers to assess how much greater the risk would be for these authors to have their words read in the same demeaning ways that their bodies are "read" every single day.

Zines are sites of unofficial literacy practices, circulating underground in what Anne Ruggles Gere calls the "extracurriculum." Gere argues that these alternative sites of literacy are important and sees the "extracurriculum as a legitimate and autonomous cultural formation that undertakes its own projects" (1994, 86). Failing to look outside the walls of the classroom for examples of reading and writing that exist apart from traditional institutions means, as Gere writes, failing to see the importance of "considering who will represent whom in what terms and in what language" (88). Failing to include these practices means inevitably telling other's stories for them.

We maintain that valuing the extracurriculum and importing it into the classroom are two different actions with decidedly different consequences. We value the extracurriculum when we preserve its context. Importing it implies removing it from its context by asking it to act within the classroom walls exactly as it did outside them. We conclude with some ways that teachers can value zines without putting zinesters at risk.

Part of what makes zines so exciting to read is the creative energy at work. These girls are playing with language and imagery in ways that are intentional, crafted, charged, and nonstandard. Like many groups that are marginalized and disempowered zinesters have taken the language in currency and subverted it for their own (political) purposes, creating what Mary Louise Pratt calls a literate art of the contact zone. Pratt defines the "contact zone" as spaces where "cultures meet, clash, and grapple with each other, often contexts of highly asymmetrical power relations" (1991, 34). The resulting texts combine elements from the hegemonic culture and its representations of those at the margins with "indigenous" elements from the marginalized community. These literate arts, Pratt suggests, "often constitute a marginalized group's point of entry into the dominant circuits of print culture" (35). In responding to representations of themselves by their classmates and what they read and see every day, zinesters access the dominant language while at the same time subverting it.

Living in the charged spaces of the contact zone, zinesters create texts that are marked by invented spelling, invented grammar, and invented language. Because their writing comes, initially, from the dominant culture, it is still recognizable as such. As readers reading from positions within this culture, we have no trouble realizing that "reel" means "real." At the same time, though, zinesters are calling attention to the fact that they have the power—within their own texts—to change the very ways they communicate ("reel" seems to mean more than "real"). In addition, because they are writing to each other, they reinforce their sense of a like-minded community by creating and upholding like-minded forms of expression. Scholars of critical literacy, such as Paulo Freire and Donald Macedo, suggest that "liberation comes only when people reclaim their language" (1987, xv). While the zinesters' use of language may appear to be incidental or, at most, playful, it actually becomes a mark of transformative social action.

What does this mean for the classroom? First, it means recognizing that students know a great deal more about language, rhetorical approaches, and audiences than most of us might think. Our students enter our classrooms already knowledgeable about ways to use discerning evidence, persuade an audience, and make a point. One way to value (rather than import) zines in the classroom is to value the knowledge our students bring with them and provide opportunities for them to demonstrate what they already know.

These opportunities might begin by allowing students the power to experiment and change language in ways that range from playful to political. This can mean assigning a single writing task that gives students this freedom or providing more latitude in general about what it means to write in the classroom. Most students have had experiences in which they have manipulated language, created secret codes, or made up nonsense songs. Calling on these extracurricular experiences and allowing students to add to them in traditional curricular settings can mean providing students with ways to reconsider their relationships to their school, their language, and their world.

Valuing the kinds of connections between language and experience that zinesters make in their writing also means reading works by authors who are experimenting with language—for example, reading the poetry of Emily Dickinson alongside Gloria Anzaldua's memoir, *Borderlands/La Frontera*. Students can learn more about craft from examples by professional writers who use language to both create and question communities of readers. Asking students to examine the form and style used by such writers is a jumping-off point, from which students can begin to think about how their own styles are affected by the ways their experiences are shaped by with the dominant culture. In addition, bringing alternative texts into the classroom is a way to value the gender and racial equity among authors that zinesters recognize as lacking in their educational experiences.

We have seen how skilled female zinesters are in representing, through language, image, and example, the ways in which they feel marginalized by their peers. While these girls have come to understand how sexism and homophobia, in particular, work to exclude them, all students share experiences of being outside the dominant culture in some way. By their very status as students, they assume a position of relative powerlessness. Having students explore their marginalized positions through autobiographical writing that grapples with what it means to be an outsider in specific, detailed ways, heads in the direction of the reflexivity the zinesters achieve. By making explicit the connections between language and experience, students can begin to consider how they resist and embrace the roles society offers them.

Finally, it is not accidental that zines are filled with images from pop culture. Movie stars, punk bands, and body piercing do not dot the edges of the zinesters' world; they center it. Often, teachers are hesitant to bring popular culture into the classroom, either because they feel it is not rigorous or academic, or because they feel they do not understand it well enough. Yet, these are the resources zinesters draw upon both to uphold and to subvert the roles and values they see modeled. Asking students to think critically about the ways they absorb and reject pop culture by bringing visual and literary icons into the classroom means asking them seriously to consider the embodied cultural messages. Zinesters successfully demonstrate the ways in which critical examination of popular culture can lead to both social action and transformation.

Conclusion

Zines are powerful, unofficial literacy practices that allow zinesters to explore issues of gender and sexual identity by writing with and against a dominant culture in ways that are experimental, political, and intentional. As in any research, there are significant issues of representation that must be examined before writing about zinesters and their work, examined in large part by considering ways in which the researcher's angles of vision both enable and constrain the sharing of context required in telling others' stories. Importing zines directly into the classroom puts already marginalized girls at even greater risk. At the same time, we can value the qualities found in zines and have students consider the ways in which their experiences, their language, and their own cultural icons establish, limit, and support their positions within the world. If we do that, we may see in our classrooms the kind of socially transforming and creative writing that zinesters so effectively circulate.

References

Alcoff, L. 1995. "The Problem of Speaking for Others." In *Who Can Speak? Authority and Critical Identity*, eds. J. Roof and R. Weigman, 97–119. Chicago: University of Illinois Press.

Block, F. L., and H. Carlip. 1998. *'zine Scene: The Do It Yourself Guide to 'zines.* New York: Girl Press.

Duncombe, S. 1997. *Zines and the Politics of Alternative Culture.* New York: Verso.

Freire, P., and D. Macedo. 1987. *Literacy: Reading the Word and the World.* South Hadley, MA: Bergin and Garvey Publishers Inc.

Gere, A. R. 1994. "Kitchen Tables and Rented Rooms: The Extra-Curriculum of Composition." *College English* (45): 75–92.

Heath, S. B. 1994. "The Functions and Uses of Literacy." In *Literacy: Language and Power*, eds. D. L. Vipond and R. Strahl, 45–57. Long Beach, CA: The State University Press.

Pratt, M. L. 1991. "Arts of the Contact Zone." *Profession* 91: 33–40.

Smith, S., and J. Watson. 1996. "Introduction." In *Getting a Life: Everyday Uses of Autobiography*, eds. S. Smith and J. Watson, 1–26. Minneapolis: University of Minnesota Press.

11

Notes from the Zine Underground

KIMRA MCPHERSON

From where I sit in my room, listening to music on a late summer after-noon, I hear a car pull up outside. A glance out my window verifies that the mail has arrived. Excited to see what has come for me, I dash barefoot out of the house and open the mailbox hatch. I peer inside, looking for envelopes, magazines—any pieces of mail with my name on them. I flip through a stack of catalogs, a few bills for my parents, and some random junk mail until I finally spot an envelope addressed to *Noodle*, c/o Kimra. The envelope feels full, with two stamps in the corner. It's no ordinary enve-lope, either; it's clearly handmade, a hybrid of magazine pages and packag-ing tape, a do-it-yourself creation. My excitement builds. Maybe a zine is waiting for me inside the envelope. Maybe somebody wants to trade their zine for mine; maybe a friend is offering feedback on my latest issue. I retreat to my room, diving into the envelope to find the latest zine from a friend in California.

Though popularized by the "riot grrrl" empowerment movement of the early nineties, zines have existed for years, ranging in form from comics of the 1950s to independent publications. These self-produced, homemade minimagazines can take on a variety of sizes and shapes, and can deal with any topic. Some are focused on solely one issue, such as rape or food or child-hood memories; others deal with different aspects of music; still others are comics. And then there are my favorites, the incredibly personal zines, the ones that allow the reader into the author's life. I always feel like I'm reading a diary when I read one of these zines; the writing is so intimate and clearly important to the writer. The spectrum of ideas that zines can encompass is endless.

I got involved with zines when I was fifteen, in the spring of my freshman year of high school. An online penpal directed me to an Internet webpage that listed twenty or so zines, complete with reviews and an address where I could write to receive each zine. Initially, the language of zining seemed foreign. What was a trade? How many stamps should I send when it says "one dollar plus stamps?" What did they mean by "half-size," "full-size," and "half-legal?" I was lost. But I kept searching through the webpage and then through the descriptions of the listed zines, printing out the pages and circling the zines I wanted to order. I couldn't even say what attracted me to each of those first zines I requested. In some cases, the zinestress (as female zine authors are often called) had written about a topic I had an interest in; in other cases, the title simply appealed to me. Whatever the reason, I was enamored with the idea of having a forum in which to write whatever I wanted to write: The thought of being able to put together my own magazine, decide its content, and design its layout intrigued me.

I began composing letters that night, writing to the authors of the zines I had selected. I requested not only their zines but also the stories of how they got involved with zining. I asked them to send their latest issues (I was amazed by the fact that some of these zines had gone on for five, seven, even fourteen issues) and their advice. Hoping that I would get at least a couple of positive replies, I dropped eleven letters into the mailbox.

About a month later, the responses started to come. My first was a postcard from a girl saying that her zine was no longer available. I remember thinking, "wow, they actually ran out of issues; these things must be really popular somewhere." But in the following weeks, I received most of the zines I had requested, and every time one arrived, I would read it cover to cover. I was becoming more and more enraptured with the world of zines, this world of photocopied, gray-toned sheets of paper with cutout clip art and articles. I realized how much work and care had gone into these products and was impressed with the honesty I found within the zine pages.

Because all of the zines I ordered and received initially were by girls—as most are—I found much in each zine to which I could relate. Sometimes just one line of poetry seemed to fit my life; at other times, an article would have me laughing out loud. I was amazed by the fact that each of these girls had so much to say. Here I was, reading zines put out by girls from all backgrounds and areas of the country, girls of all different ages with widely varying opinions on a huge range of topics; suddenly, I wanted to be a part of the movement. Zining, to me, seemed like a very empowering thing: I would be able to take whatever I was thinking and put it on paper. I could handwrite or type or word-process this writing however I pleased; I would be able to lay out the pages in any way I wanted, form the zine into any size. I could make a pocket-sized zine or a collection of stapled full sheets of paper. And I could devote the entire thing to myself, my opinions, my life.

This exciting underground network of young women doing zines seemed to me like a cross between a literary discussion circle and a support group, a place where all ideas were welcomed and all opinions both respected and open to debate. Here were young women, opinionated writers like myself, all wanting to make their thoughts known and voices heard. All of them offered advice to me on how to get started: "Write what means something to you. Write what you care about; write things that are important to you as a person." I wasn't sure if I had that kind of honesty in me, but, inspired, I sat down and started to write.

I now look back on my first issue of *Noodle,* distributed in July 1997, as many look back on their first-day-of school pictures: A certain amount of pride in how much I've grown and changed since then is muddled with the embarrassment of the bad haircut or horrible outfit that is immortalized on film. For my first zine venture, I had wanted to put out a product that would honestly reflect where I was at that point in my life, but I was afraid to dig too deeply into myself. When I found my confidence in my zining ability waning, I wrote several more times for advice from the girls with whom I had continued to correspond. They were always eager to help me, the newcomer to the scene, with my project. And every time I'd write, I always heard the cry again: "Write what you care about." I was determined to try.

Physically putting together the first issue of *Noodle* was another challenge. I learned how—and how not—to assemble and copy a zine (layout is trickier than it looks). I learned what does and does not make a good background for articles. I learned that photocopying pictures sometimes doesn't work as well as I'd like. I found I enjoyed rubber-cementing the pieces of my zine to their backgrounds, watching the zine become a concrete product before my eyes.

And so, after three months of thought and work, *Noodle* was born. "As I was reading, this little nagging voice in the back of my head kept saying to me, 'you could do this, too,' . . . I mean, I have lots of stuff to express, so isn't this one of the best ways to do it?" I wrote in my introduction to *Noodle* No. 1. "Be sure to let me know what you think," I asked my audience, "but be kind to me! I'm just a semi-clueless budding zinestress. . . ." Without delving too deeply into my personal feelings, my first issue was an overview of the things I experienced over the months I worked on the zine. It contained stories from my civics class, ways to have fun at the mall, and a long article about why my ninth-grade health class had failed miserably. The more I worked at it, the more secure I became in putting my work out to an audience that I didn't really know. In fact, I was able to be more confident because only a few, select, people whom I knew in real life would be reading my zine; most of my audience was unknown, presented to me only as a name and address on a brightly colored envelope in my mailbox. Writing for this unknown audience made me feel as if I were writing only to myself. As I wrote, I could pretend that since I didn't know my readers, they didn't exist.

I received a number of letters from those who read *Noodle* No. #1, both complimenting my efforts and offering suggestions on what I could do to improve. Because of this feedback—and because, frankly, I liked putting the zine together so much—I decided to continue. I began to open myself up in my writing, letting my emotions come through more and more. Writing for the zine was like asking myself questions—the difference was that by letting this zinestress network read the questions I was posing, I could actually get some answers. Being a member of the zine community has allowed me to, in a very safe manner, express my feelings and put them out for a selective piece of the public to read. Though I don't know them, I trust the girls who read my zines because they, too, put their hearts on paper and send their words and zines around the country, never knowing or having a secure idea of what the reaction to their innermost feelings will be. Anybody who can consciously tell deep thoughts to an unknown audience and is willing to accept feedback on these thoughts is worthy of seeing my own.

The zine scene thrives on feedback. Since it is centered almost entirely around the mail system, zine people are constantly "doing mail": reading the letters and zines they've received, writing their own responses, filling requests for zines, sending out copies to potential traders and readers, and giving feedback and advice to new zinesters. The extremely popular and well known zines can receive hundreds upon hundreds of pieces of mail; my own zine is not big enough for me to have experienced anything like that. But I still eagerly check my mail for weeks after I send out each issue, always wondering who will hear about and request my zine and who, of the people I've already written to, will respond.

Mail is time-consuming, and with the cost of stamps added to the already high cost of actually photocopying the zines, zining can be expensive. I read a survey once that was designed to pinpoint whether the survey taker was a qualified candidate for zinedom or not; the first question asked if I, as a zinestress, would expect to "make a little money, break even, or lose money." The fact is, unless you have post office connections or a copy machine at home, zining is very costly. The cost, however, is nothing when compared to the self-fulfillment and understanding that zining provide—zining is beyond priceless; it becomes a necessary form of communication. And for girls who do not have a nearby support network for personal issues, the zine community is truly a family.

In my written correspondence with other zinestresses, I have found that many of them wish they had begun their zining earlier in life. Some did not begin until high school. After realizing how much zines and the zine community had helped them, they wished that they had found that kind of support to help them through junior high or middle school as they worked toward discovering their personalities and who they wanted to be. Having an outlet for these feelings of self-doubt and self-discovery is a huge benefit of zining; the zine movement in itself promotes that kind of inner growth. Because zines are sent out into an environment of empathy, understanding, and debate, zinestresses and their readers can explore and identify with issues of change, and also bear witness to amazing healing and discovery, to self-realization and self-acceptance.

Therein lies the purest power of zines: their ability to be intensely personal and yet unite young women as they adjust to changes in their lives and discover what they stand for. Zines allow for open discussion on any and all topics; they provide the chance to take a stand on any issues that are important to the writer. They provide a coping mechanism and a forum for venting about the pressures and joys of daily life. Granted, zinemaking is a very self-absorbed process. Essentially, each zinestress is assembling a photocopied booklet all about herself and her opinions; it's all about the writer. And often, this is exactly what the zinestress needs: a chance to be vain and talk about herself to a receptive, interested audience.

Always growing and always changing, always evolving and always enduring: Such is the zine movement among young women today. As they grow in popularity, thanks in part to the testimonials of girls who have gained confidence from the opportunities for expression that zining provides, zines have attracted wider attention. More mainstream authors have begun to write about them in articles or books, hoping that their writing will reach and inspire girls to start zining.

One such publication is 'zine Scene: The Do It Yourself Guide to 'zines (1998), cowritten by Francesca Lia Block of the Weetzie Bat series and Hillary Carlip of Girl Power. Everything about zines is explained here, from how to get them, to how to lay out and copy a zine, to hints on content and copyright information. In November 1998, I participated in a roundtable discussion and book signing with Hillary, Sara McCool of the zine Sourpuss, and Ciara LaVelle of Starshine. Speaking to an audience of readers and writers of all ages, we discussed and analyzed our own zining experiences and what being a part of this movement has done for us. I realized that day how much zining has taught me about the way I communicate, and, perhaps more importantly, how to be really honest in communication. Zines have also given me a chance to experiment with different styles of writing. I can try something original and untested, print it in my zine, and gather responses from my network of zine peers. For example, if I hadn't found an outlet for my poetry in my zine, I am sure I wouldn't write nearly as much of it as I now do. In addition, zines have made me a more secure and confident writer. Though I'm still wary of sharing my writing with those I know, the positive responses I've received from other zinestresses have made me more able to do so. As zinestress Sara McCool noted during the discussion, because zines are unstructured, they allow their editors to take risks they may not normally take. Hillary Carlip added that zines are "raw and real," providing young women with the opportunity to "claim their own power without being told what to do."

Zine writers grow with their zines. The writing quality improves, the originality improves, and the amount of expression put into the work improves. When a woman from the crowd asked if we were better writers because of zines, all three of us said yes. Looking back on an issue I did a few months ago—one I was so proud of—and comparing it to my most recent *Noodle,* I can definitely see the change. Putting the issues together, from first to most current, is like assembling volumes of personal journals that reflect the last two years of my life. I can always look back on those zines to see where I was at the moment I wrote an article, realize how I felt as I designed the page, and analyze my mood as I wrote my introduction to each of my zines. Little time capsules, they are, little pieces of me.

For *'zine Scene,* Hillary and Francesca rated the material they received on what they called the "Chill-o-Meter"—the more a piece gave them chills, the more likely it was to be used. Zine writers who dare to put their opinions on paper and pass them out to peers, who take the risk of voicing controversial opinions and taking a firm stand on issues, who chance revealing the most intimate details of their lives to an audience they barely know (or may not know at all) are all vying for spots on their readers' "Chill-o-Meters." When a zine evokes emotion from me, I know that zinestress has done her job. Unlike the writer of that first tentative *Noodle,* I now strive to do that same thing in my writing: I want to be so intensely personal that I give somebody chills. But most of all, I want to write my zine for me. "Write what you care about," I was always told, and in so doing, I've recorded some of the most powerful, influential moments in my life.

Every time I tell others about my zine, a little part of me still catches my breath to realize how cool it is to be a part of a huge underground movement. Every time I receive a response to *Noodle,* every time somebody debates a thought or opinion I voiced, every time peers tells me how my writing helped or haunted them, I'm reminded of the strong network of zine women of which I am a member. I know that no matter what I have to say, somebody will read it and care. And I know that, years from now, I'll be able to look back on my zine and smile; I'll laugh, and I'll cry, and I'll be reminded once again of the power of expression that *Noodle*—and all zines—inherently hold.

Reference

Block, F. L., and H. Carlip. 1998. *'zine Scene: The Do It Yourself Guide to 'zines.* New York: Girl Press.

PART VI

Selected Texts and Other Resources

[E]ducators can help women develop their own authentic voices if they emphasize connection over separation, understanding and acceptance over assessment, and collaboration over debate; if they accord respect to and allow time for the knowledge that emerges from first hand experience; if instead of imposing their own expectations and arbitrary requirements, they encourage students to evolve their own patterns of work based on the problems they are pursuing.
—M. F. BELENKY, B. M. CLINCHY, N. R. GOLDBERGER, AND J. M. TARULE, *Women's Ways of Knowing*

12

Gender Fare

In Support of Gender Equity in Literacy Learning

LINDA CULLUM

This annotated bibliography covers English-language sources—including books, journal articles, ERIC documents, and Internet sources—that focus on the general topic of gender equity and schooling, as well as sources that address gender issues in adolescence and in literacy learning. The sources are separated into seven classifications: gender and schooling; adolescents, gender roles, and society; adolescents, gender, and literacy learning; boys—the understudied majority; gender-fair approaches to literacy learning; adolescents, gender, and visual literacy; and adolescents, gender, and computer literacy. International Standard Book Numbers (ISBNs) are given for books and appear after the publisher.

Gender and Schooling

The AAUW Report: How Schools Shortchange Girls. 1992. Washington, DC: The American Association of University Women.

Prepared by the Wellesley College Center for Research on Women, this report carefully documents how our educational system shortchanges girls through classroom and testing practices. Numerous statistics make a compelling case for the need for educational reform to correct this "evaded curriculum." Forty recommendations for increasing gender fairness in the schools conclude the report.

Backes, J. S. 1994. "Bridging the Gender Gap: Self-concept in the Middle Grades." *Schools in the Middle* 3 (summer): 19–23.

Reports on the results of a self-esteem questionnaire ("How I Feel About Myself") given to over twelve hundred students in a North Dakota middle school. Findings confirm the prevailing belief that adolescent females' self-concepts are much lower than those of their male peers. A copy of the survey instrument is included.

Bailey, S. M. 1996. "Shortchanging Girls and Boys." *Educational Leadership* 53 (5): 75–79.

Written by the primary author of the 1992 AAUW report *How Schools Shortchange Girls,* this essay encourages educators to review their own possibly sexist behaviors.

Cohen, J., and S. Blanc. 1996. *Girls in the Middle: Working to Succeed in School.* Washington, DC: AAUW Educational Foundation. ISBN 1-87992-215-0.

A follow-up to the AAUW report *How Schools Shortchange Girls,* this report summarizes a research study that examined adolescent girls' reactions to the educational reform programs in their middle schools. Six schools across the country were studied in order to capture a range of geographical settings, economic conditions, and ethnic backgrounds. A video report is available.

Davidson, A. L. 1996. *Making and Molding Identity in Schools: Student Narratives on Race, Gender and Academic Engagement.* Binghampton, NY: State University of New York Press. ISBN 0-791-43081-2.

Part of the series *Power, Social Identity, and Education,* edited by Lois Weis, this work offers case studies that illuminate the perspectives of twelve sophomores of various ethnicities (African American, Euro-American, Latina/Latino, and Vietnamese) in California high schools. They reveal the large extent to which daily interactions and experiences within school settings shape adolescents' racial and ethnic identities and affect their academic engagement.

Debold, E. 1995. "Helping Girls Survive the Middle Grades." *Principal* 74 (3): 22–24.

Offering another perspective on girls' drop in self-esteem by age twelve, this essay links the drop with increased stress, depression, and suicide attempts in adolescent girls and provides strategies for helping girls resist strict adherence to cultural roles and expectations.

Diller, A., M. Ayim, and K. Morgan. 1996. *Gender Questions in Education: Theory, Pedagogy, and Politics.* Boulder, CO: Westview Press. ISBN 0-813-32563-3.

Written by three philosophers of education, this is a useful introduction to the debates surrounding the role of gender in educational practices, policy making, and theory.

Eder, D., S. Parker, and C. C. Evans. 1995. *School Talk: Gender and Adolescent Culture.* New Brunswick, NJ: Rutgers University Press. ISBN 0-813-52178-5.

The authors spent three years in a midwestern middle school listening to what eleven- to fourteen-year-olds said to each other, in and out of the classroom. Findings reveal the persistence of gender and social stereotyping in American culture. Suggestions for enhancing the quality of the middle school experience are offered.

"Gender Bias: Recent Research and Interventions." 1996. *New Jersey Research Bulletin,* 22 (spring). ERIC, ED 404466.

Focusing on grades five through twelve, this annotated bibliography describes fourteen publications about recent research on gender bias and interventions aimed at reducing such bias in schools.

Hamner, T. J. 1996. *The Gender Gap in Schools: Girls Losing Out.* New York: Enslow Publishers. ISBN 0-89490-718-2.

Part of a series aimed at young adult readers, this work combines facts and statistics with accessible language to show that girls do not always get equal treatment in schools. Includes a list of helpful organizations that work to counter sexism in schools.

Hostile Hallways: The AAUW Survey on Sexual Harrassment in America's Schools. 1993. Annapolis Junction, MD: AAUW Sales Office. ERIC, ED 356186.

Presents the findings of an AAUW survey conducted by Louis Harris and Associates to ascertain the nature of sexual harassment in our nation's schools. Over sixteen hundred public school students in grades eight through eleven across America were polled, and a startling four out of five students (male and female) reported that they had been the target of some sort of harassment in their school lives.

Kenway, J. 1998. *Answering Back: Girls, Boys, and Feminism in Schools.* New York: Routledge. ISBN 0-41518-917.

An Australian scholar, Kenway has taken the next step in gender-equity research by describing what happens in schools when feminist ideas come in contact with the everyday life in schools. She examines how teachers address gender issues; how students respond; and what kinds of educational reform programs garner the most support.

LaFrance, M. 1991. "School for Scandal: Different Educational Experiences for Females and Males." *Gender and Education* 3: 3–13.

Draws on recent classroom studies to show that expectations for boys and girls still differ greatly: Boys are encouraged to participate actively and often disruptively, while girls are taught to be quiet listeners.

Laskey, L., and C. Beavis, eds. 1996. *Schooling and Sexualities: Teaching for a Positive Sexuality.* Victoria, Australia: Deakin Centre for Education and Change.

Includes a number of provocative essays, including ones that address homophobia, harassment, and sexual violence.

"Martha's Gender Equity in Education Page." Available on the Internet at http://www.crpc.rice.edu/CRPG/GT/mborrow/GenderEquity/gend.site.html

The author, a middle school science teacher, has designed a website to address the lack of gender equity in education. The site offers a number of compelling statistics; current and frequently updated information; and a number of links, including one to full-text articles in *The ALAN Review.*

Matthews, C. E., W. Binkley, A. Crisp, and K. Gregg. 1997–1998. "Challenging Gender Bias in Fifth Grade." *Educational Leadership* 55 (4) (December–January): 54–57.

Contributes to the growing number of studies that document ways in which teachers often unwittingly contribute to inequitable classroom environments.

McCracken, N. M., and others. 1996. "Resisting Gender Binding in the Middle School." *Voices from the Middle* 3 (February): 4–10.

Discusses gender issues in language arts and science classrooms and offers practical strategies for combatting gender stereotyping.

Murphy, P., and C. Gipps, eds. 1996. *Equity in the Classroom: Towards Effective Pedagogy for Girls and Boys.* London: Taylor & Francis. ISBN 0-75070-541-8.

First presented at a 1995 UNESCO international colloquium focused on the theme "Is There a Pedagogy for Girls?" these papers cover a range of current themes, including the single-sex classroom, strategies for gender-fair teaching, and gender and literacy learning.

Olivares, R. A., and N. Rosenthal. 1992. *Gender Equity and Classroom Experiences: A Review of Research.* ERIC, ED 366701.

This troubling report reviews research on how gender inequality is learned and accepted at home and then reinforced in schools. More positively, the study concludes that nonsexist curricula can and do make a difference in children's gender equity values.

Phelan, P., A. L. Davidson, and H. C. Yu. 1998. *Adolescents' Worlds: Negotiating Family, Peers, and School.* New York: Teachers College Press. ISBN 0-8077-3682-1.

Seven case studies that offer a fascinating glimpse into the struggles of adolescence and students' ongoing attempts to negotiate their multiple worlds.

Sadker, D., and M. Sadker. 1994. *Failing at Fairness: How America's Schools Cheat Girls.* New York: Scribner's Sons. ISBN 0-68480-073X.

A germinal publication that continues the ground-breaking work on gender fairness that the Sadkers began twenty-five years ago with their first book-length publication, *Sexism in Schools.* This is a comprehensive look at the "hidden lessons" of inequality and sexism that our children learn in school every day. It provides a historical overview of women's education in this culture; describes the ways that boys are also disadvantaged by gender stereotyping; and offers an excellent list of recommended readings.

Separated by Sex: A Critical Look at Single-Sex Education for Girls. 1998. Annapolis Junction, MD: AAUW Sales Office. ISBN 1-879922-16-9.

Reports on a one-day roundtable meeting that examined research on K–12 single-sex education. The consensus was that no conclusive evidence exists to support the claim that single-sex education is better for girls. Four roundtable papers are included, along with a literature review.

Shaw, J. 1995. *Education, Gender, and Anxiety.* London: Taylor & Francis. ISBN 0-74840-102-4.

British sociologist Shaw revisits persistent gender-equity and schooling issues and stresses the need to pay attention to the unconscious processes that school settings reinforce. She also considers the efficacy of single-sex education.

Sheffer, S. 1995. *A Sense of Self: Listening to Home-Schooled Adolescent Girls.* Portsmouth, NH: Boynton/Cook Publishers. ISBN 0-86709-405-2.

This project investigates whether the same drop in self-esteem is evidenced in adolescent girls who are educated outside of the school system. Editor of the journal *Growing Without Schooling,* Sheffer points to many differences between the girls in her study and their traditionally educated peers, including greater self-reliance, reflexiveness, and sense of self.

Shmurak, C. B., and T. M. Ratkiff. 1993. *Gender Equity and Gender Bias in the Middle School Classroom.* ERIC, ED 363548.

The authors visited eighty classes in ten middle schools in central Connecticut in search of evidence of either gender equity or gender bias. Surprisingly, math classes in the sample showed the most equity, while language arts classes revealed the greatest male domination. Relates striking examples of the various forms of sexism found.

Shortchanging Girls, Shortchanging America: A Nationwide Poll to Assess Self Esteem, Educational Experiences, Interest in Math and Science, and Career Aspirations of Girls and Boys Ages 9–15. 1991, 1994. Washington, DC: American Association of University Women. ISBN 1-87992-202-9.

Describes the results of the two surveys administered to thousands of children across America, all of which point to a dramatic drop in self-confidence in girls as they approach adolescence. There is also a separate ERIC document, *Shortchanging Hispanic Girls* (ED 387557), that analyzes the same data with a focus on Latinas.

Shortchanging Girls, Shortchanging America: A Call to Action. 1992. Washington, DC: American Association of University Women. ISBN 1-879922-00-2.

Reviews the early steps of the AAUW's Initiative for Educational Equity. Discussed first is the initial survey sent to three thousand fourth- through tenth-grade students to explore the impact of gender on such matters as self-esteem, career aspirations, and educational experiences. The second focus is on the 1991 roundtable meeting that was held to discuss the findings of the survey.

Stitt, B. A. 1994. *Gender Equity in Education: An Annotated Bibliography.* Carbondale: Southern Illinois University Press. ISBN 0-80931-937-3.

Hundreds of books, articles, videos, and curriculum guides are annotated in this invaluable tool for educators. Each entry provides a short description of content, the age group to which the resource applies, and ordering information.

Thorne, B. 1993. *Gender Play: Girls and Boys in School.* New Brunswick, NJ: Rutgers University Press. ISBN 0-81351-923-3.

Barrie Thorne, a preeminent scholar of language and gender, turns her attention to the public school setting in this ethnographic study of gender relations in childhood and adolescence. The result is a highly readable and insightful examination of the different cultural experiences of growing up male or female in today's society.

Tshumy, R. D. 1995. "What Do We Know About Girls? Ensuring Gender Equity in the Classroom." *NASSP Bulletin* 79 (November): 58–61.
    Speaking primarily to secondary school administrators, the author urges that school personnel acknowledge the turmoil of adolescence for girls and encourage their voices, rather than their compliance, in classrooms.

Weis, L., and M. Fine. 1993. *Beyond Silenced Voices: Class, Race, and Gender in United States Schools.* Albany: State University of New York Press. ISBN 0-79141-286-5.
    Presents sixteen essays, including several with a specific gender focus. See especially R. W. Connell's "Disruptions: Improper Masculinities and Schooling" and Linda K. Christian-Smith's "Voices of Resistance: Young Women Readers of Romance Fiction."

Wrigley, J., ed. 1992. *Education and Gender Equality.* London: Taylor & Francis. ISBN 1-85000-946-5.
    This collection grew out of a special issue of *Sociology of Education* that addresses equity matters in schools and universities.

Adolescents, Gender Roles, and Society

Barbieri, M. 1995. *Sounds from the Heart: Learning to Listen to Girls.* Portsmouth, NH: Heinemann. ISBN 0-435-08843-2.
    Winner of NCTE's James Britton Research Award and Delta Kappa Gamma's Educator's Award, this is a far-reaching case study about a group of adolescent schoolgirls and the role of literacy in their lives. Both parents and teachers will benefit from reading this insightful yet highly practical approach to ensuring that girls' voices are heard in our homes and classrooms.

Brown, L. M., and C. Gilligan. 1992. *Meeting at the Crossroads: Women's Psychology and Girls' Development.* Cambridge, MA: Harvard University Press. ISBN 0-674-56464-2.
    In order to explore girls' development and its implication for the psychology of women, the authors interviewed nearly one hundred girls between the ages of seven and eighteen at the Laurel School for Girls in Cleveland, Ohio. The result is this fascinating discussion that blends generalizations about the struggles of female adolescents with case studies of individual girls.

Ms. Foundation for Women. 1998. *Girls Seen and Heard: 52 Lessons for Our Daughters.* New York: Putnum. ISBN 0-87477-926x.

Aimed at girls aged nine to fifteen and the women in their lives, this book sets out collaborative assignments designed to encourage girls to believe in themselves, to explore their options, and to learn how to command respect.

Ornstein, P. 1994. *Schoolgirls: Young Women, Self-Esteem, and the Confidence Gap.* Washington, DC: American Association of University Women. ISBN 0-385-42576-7.

This engaging study is must reading for both parents and educators of young women. Sponsored by the AAUW, Ornstein spent a year with African American, Latina, and Anglo-American eighth graders in two California schools. She offers a detailed and compelling glimpse into the world of adolescence. Among her findings are that the passage into adolescence is marked by a girl's loss of confidence in herself and her abilities, and that the media and our educational system are shortchanging young women.

Pipher, M. B. 1995. *Reviving Ophelia: Saving the Selves of Adolescent Girls.* New York: Putman. ISBN 0-34539-282-5.

Clinical psychologist Pipher paints a frightening portrait of female adolescence in today's society. Using case studies and lively, accessible prose, she shows how the culture "poisons" its young women by depriving them of self-esteem, pitting them against one another, and establishing an unattainable version of ideal beauty. She also offers suggestions for helping girls resist social pressures.

Rhode, D. L. 1996. *Speaking of Sex.* Cambridge, MA: Harvard University Press. ISBN 0-67483-177-2.

A law professor at Stanford University, Rhode explores sex-based inequalities that exist in our culture and examines the inadequacy of current public policy to combat this problem.

Rothenberg, D. 1995. *Supporting Girls in Early Adolescence.* ERIC Digest. Urbana, IL: ERIC Clearinghouse on Elementary and Early Childhood Education. ERIC, ED 386331.

Available in full-text form on the Internet, this study considers factors—both in and out of the classroom—that may contribute to adolescent girls' drop in self-esteem, and makes specific recommendations for counteracting these factors.

Shockley, B., J. B. Allen, and B. Michalove. 1995. *Engaging Families: Connecting Home and School Literacy Communities.* Portsmouth, NH: Heinemann. ISBN 0-435-08845-9.

Offers practical suggestions about how parents and schools can work together to develop partnerships for promoting literacy learning. Appended materials include an extensive source bibliography and a model family reading journal.

Adolescents, Gender, and Literacy Learning

Allen, J. 1995. *It's Never Too Late: Leading Adolescents to Lifelong Literacy.* Portsmouth, NH: Heinemann. ISBN 0-435-08839-4.

Describes Allen's action research, done while teaching reading to at-risk high school students, and offers a compassionate look at students for whom school has not been a positive experience. Includes a detailed guide to creating a literate environment and a lifelong reading habit.

"Allowing Boys and Girls to Become More Fully Human: An Interview with Judy Logan." 1995. *Quarterly of the National Writing Project and the Center for the Study of Writing and Literacy* 17 (2) (spring): 12–14.

Middle school teacher Judy Logan has long been a vocal advocate of gender equity in the classroom, both in her writing and in her daily classroom practices. This interview focuses specifically on gender differences in students' choices of writing topics.

Alvermann, D. E. and others. 1997. *Adolescents' Negotiations of Out-of-School Reading Discussions.* Reading Research Report No. 77. College Park, MD: National Reading Research Center. ERIC, ED 403551.

An ethnographic study of voluntary "read and talk" clubs that met weekly in a library after school, the data—including daily literacy activity logs kept by the participants—suggests that the clubs were a positive social outlet and increased time spent reading.

Alvermann, D. E., and others. 1996. *Interrupting Gendered Discursive Practices in Classroom Talk About Texts: Easy to Think About, Difficult to Do.* Reading Research Report No. 54. Athens, GA: National Reading Research Center. ERIC, ED 396256.

This ethnography focuses on the importance, and difficulty, of teachers' awareness of gender dynamics during text-based classroom discussions. Data was collected from three sites: seventh- and eighth-grade language arts classes and a graduate-level class on literacy instruction.

Blair, H. 1998. "They Left Their Genderprints: The Voice of Girls in Text." *Language Arts* 75 (1) (January): 11–18.

Using the concept of "genderprints," Blair shows how the writings of a group of eighth-grade girls were infused with the multiple realities of their lives as young women in a working-class neighborhood.

Carlip, H., ed. 1995. *Girl Power: Young Women Speak Out: Personal Writings from Teenage Girls.* New York: Warner Books.

A very popular collection of stories, letters, poems, and notes from girls aged thirteen to nineteen, representing a variety of backgrounds and perspectives.

Cherland, M. R. 1994. *Private Practices: Girls Reading Fiction and Constructing Identity.* London and Bristol, PA: Taylor & Francis. ISBN: 0-7484-022-5X.

This detailed case study of the reading practices of seven sixth-grade Canadian girls, all of whom were avid readers, reveals the highly gendered nature of their reading practices and uncovers, schools' "hidden curriculum." It is part of the *Critical Perspectives on Literacy and Education* series.

"Closing the Gender Gap: Literacy for Women and Girls." 1990. *United Nations Chronicle* 27 (1) (March): 56–58.

UNESCO estimates that two-thirds of the estimated 965 million adult illiterates around the world are female, and that nearly half of all women in developing nations do not know how to read or write. The report addresses this crisis and describes efforts being made by UN-sponsored organizations.

Commeyras, M., and others. 1997. "Educators' Stances Toward Gender Issues in Literacy." Paper presented as part of the American Educational Research Association at the annual meeting, Chicago, IL, March 24. ERIC, ED 407669.

Reports on results of a survey designed to ascertain attitudes toward and interest in gender issues in literacy education. The results of the survey, which was administered to over fifteen hundred K–12 teachers, reading specialists, and administrators, indicated a strong desire to stay with traditional, "appropriate" language arts curricula in schools.

Evans, K. S., D. Alvermann, and P. L. Anders. 1998. "Literature Discussion Groups: An Examination of Gender Roles." *Reading Research and Instruction.* 37 (2) (winter): 107–122.

Highlights the experiences of three female middle school students who were members of peer-led literature discussion groups that examined notions of empowerment, student voice, and silence.

Finders, M. J. 1997. *Just Girls: Hidden Literacies and Life in Junior High.* New York: Teachers College Press. ISBN 0-8077-3560-4.

Finders studied the role of literacy in the development of five academically successful middle school girls in the Midwest. She reports a range of literacy events, from academic work to reading teen magazines and writing graffiti. An earlier, less expanded version of this study can be found in *Written Communication* (January 1996, 93–129). This book is part of the Language and Literacy Series edited by D. S. Strickland and C. Genishi.

Fox, M. 1993. "Men Who Weep, Boys Who Dance: The Gender Agenda Between the Lines in Children's Literature." *Language Arts* 70 (February): 84–88.

Presents further examples of female passivity and general inferiority in children's literature and calls for change.

"Genderizing the Curriculum." 1999. *English Journal* 88 (January): 3.

All of the articles published in the January 1999 issue of *English Journal,* the NCTE journal for secondary teachers, were devoted to perspectives on gender and the English/language arts curriculum.

Gilbert, P. 1992. "The Story So Far: Gender, Literacy, and Social Regulation." *Gender and Education* 4: 185–199.

Examines the extent to which literacy education is a gendered practice and calls for increased critical scrutiny.

Hudson, J. W. 1994. "Engaging Resistant Writers Through Zines in the Classroom." ERIC, ED 373352.

Describes the underground phenomenon of zines and explores their applicability to the language arts classroom.

Hunter, A., and others. 1993. "Considering Gender Issues in the Teaching of English." *English Journal* 82 (March): 87–89.

What would you answer to the question "What work has been the most helpful to you in considering gender issues in the teaching of English?" This essay tells you how seven practicing teachers responded and gives citations for their recommendations.

Jones, P. 1994. "A to Z and In-Between: New Magazines for Young Adults." *Voice of Youth Advocates* 16 (February): 352–358.

This review suggests forty-eight magazines appropriate for young adults, including zines.

Kelly, J. A. 1995. *Exploring Attitudes Toward Gender in the Language Arts Classroom.* ERIC, ED 380800.

Twenty-six female and male seventh graders were studied in an attempt to determine if exposing middle school students to nonstereotypical protagonists in the books they read affects their gender-biased attitudes. The research project and its findings are described in detail.

Livingston-Webber, J. 1994. *How Sassy Are Grrrl Zines?* ERIC, ED 376510.

An overview of this girls' literacy movement that contains a selective list of zines and considers the genre's applicability to the classroom.

Millard, E. 1997. "Differently Literate: Gender Identity and the Construction of the Developing Reader." *Gender and Education* 9 (1): 31–48.

This study of 255 British children traces three specific areas of influence that shape the attitudes and expectations of adolescent reading: family, friendship groups, and school peer groups. Identifies patterns of gender differences in the reading experience.

Mitchell, D. 1996. "Approaching Race and Gender Issues in the Context of the Language Arts Classroom." *English Journal* 85 (December): 77–81.

Presents over twenty-five activities designed to engage secondary language arts students in race and gender issues.

Orellana, M. F. 1994. *Literacy as a Gendered Social Practice in Two Bilingual Classrooms.* ERIC, ED 387386.

Considers gender's role in shaping students' willingness to participate in literacy activities in schools. It also offers an often-overlooked perspective, in that the study was conducted in two Spanish-English bilingual classrooms, led by a Spanish-speaking teacher, within a predominantly Latino working-class neighborhood.

Peirce, K. 1993. *Socialization of Teenage Girls Through Teen-Magazine Fiction: The Making of a New Woman or an Old Lady?* ERIC, ED 361732.

In order to investigate the socialization messages sent by popular adolescent girls' magazines, this study analyzed 104 fiction stories that appeared in *Seventeen* and *Teen* magazines over a five-year period. Findings show that the stories overwhelmingly supported traditional social constructions of gender.

Pottorff, D. D., and others. 1996. "Gender Perception of Elementary and Middle School Students About Literacy at School and Home." *Journal of Research and Development in Education* 29 (summer): 203–11.

This study confirms literacy research that suggests that students view reading and writing as female activities.

Rutledge, M. 1997. "Reading the Subtext on Gender." *Educational Leadership* 54 (April): 71–73.

Rutledge, president of a consulting firm that specializes in organizational change, describes the Vermont Equity Project, which she developed as a means of teaching cultural literacy in schools. She also offers practical suggestions for helping students to understand the cultural messages that shape the ways they see themselves.

Schulteis, C. 1990. *A Study of the Relationship Between Gender and Reading Preferences in Adolescents.* ERIC, ED 367376.

Reports on the findings of a survey distributed to approximately 240 suburban eleventh graders. Confirming many earlier studies, the findings show that females spend more time reading than do males, and that both genders report preferring books with male protagonists. Interesting tables are appended, including male and female choices of magazines and newspaper sections.

Smith, S. A. 1997. "Book Club Is 'Da Bomb': Early Adolescent Girls Engage with Texts, Transactions, and Talk." Paper presented at American Educational Research Association annual meeting, Chicago, IL, March 24. ERIC, ED 407650.

Reports on an after-school book club whose members were eight sixth-grade girls of various ethnic backgrounds. The club was found to be an important and liberating means for the girls to negotiate identities and responses, away from the pressures of school and issues of gender.

Waff, D. 1995. "Romance in the Classroom: Inviting Discourse on Gender and Power." *Quarterly of the National Writing Project and the Center for the Study of Writing and Literacy* 17 (spring): 15–18.

Waff offers an often-overlooked perspective by addressing gender issues in special education classes. She describes her use of journal writing and discussion that focuses on questions of gender and power in a patriarchal culture.

Boys—The Understudied Majority

Alloway, N., and P. Gilbert. 1997. "Boys and Literacy: Lessons from Australia." *Gender and Education* 9 (1): 49–58.

Research done in Australia that demonstrates ways in which literacy can be constructed by schools to run counter to the culture's messages about what it means to be masculine.

Connell, R. W. 1996. "Teaching the Boys: New Research on Masculinity and Gender Strategies for Schools." *Teachers College Record* 98 (2) (winter): 206–35.

This compelling essay offers a framework for understanding gender issues in boys' education; summarizes new masculinity research; and considers how schooling contributes to the making of boys' identities in this culture.

Davies, B. 1997. "Constructing and Deconstructing Masculinities Through Critical Literacy." *Gender and Education* 9 (1): 9–30.

Coming out of Australia, where so much important work on young males and literacy is being done, Davies scrutinizes the way that literacy is often taught in patriarchal cultures and makes concrete suggestions for change.

Gurian, M. 1998. *A Fine Young Man: What Parents, Mentors, and Educators Can Do to Shape Adolescent Boys into Exceptional Men.* New York: Putnam. ISBN 0-87477-919-7.

Gurian, the author of a successful guide to raising healthy young boys, runs against the current of most contemporary gender research here by positing a biological basis for many male behavioral traits, such as aggression. He urges readers to understand and nurture this seriously "undernourished" population.

Hall, C., and M. Coles. 1997. "Gendered Readings: Helping Boys Develop as Critical Readers." *Gender and Education* 9: 61–68.

This intriguing report on the reading habits of British boys and girls, ages ten through fourteen, argues that boys in particular need to be encouraged to understand how they have been socially constructed as readers.

Martino, W. 1995. "Deconstructing Masculinity in the English Classroom: A Site for Reconstituting Gendered Subjectivity." *Gender and Education* 7 (2): 205–220.

An important voice in the conversation about gender studies and masculinity, Martino offers practical suggestions for valorizing alternate subject positions for high school males in the English classroom.

Nechamkin, K. "Educational Equity for Boys." Available on the Internet at http://www.escape.com/~knechamk/educ1.htm

This site's author presents selected statistics and observations to support his contention that boys are being seriously neglected by our educational system. He calls for "male-positive motivation and reinforcement."

Pollack, W. 1998. *Real Boys: Rescuing Our Sons from the Myths of Boyhood.* New York: Random House. ISBN 0-375-50131-2.

Pollack—a clinical psychologist and codirector of the Center for Men at the Harvard Medical Center—confronts what he terms the "boy code" in American society, which dictates conformity to the cultural stereotype of what constitutes masculinity. He advises parents to combat gender typing by talking, listening to, and nurturing their sons.

Salisbury, J., and D. Jackson. 1996. *Challenging Macho Values: Ways of Working with Boys in Secondary Schools.* London: Taylor & Francis. ISBN 0-75070-484-5.

An excellent, practical guide designed by two British teachers committed to expanding boys' concepts of what it means to be a man in today's society. They offer numerous lesson plans addressing such issues as media images, language use, and sexual harassment.

Sewell, T. 1997. *Black Masculinites and Schooling: How Black Boys Survive Modern Schooling.* Staffordshire, England: Trentham Books Ltd. ISBN 1-85856-040-3.

This highly theoretical investigation into the development and regulation of black masculinities offers an important perspective on an often-overlooked topic. While the focus of this study is on male students of African Caribbean heritage in Great Britain, many of the findings are applicable to young black males in general.

Smith, R. 1995. "Schooling and the Formation of Male Students' Gender Identities." *Theory and Research in Social Education* 24: 54–70.

Smith claims that we have a very limited understanding of the ways in which masculinity is socially constructed, and in particular of what role schooling plays in this process. He presents a compelling argument for why the young males—especially white males—in our classrooms need attention and not reductive generalizations.

Way, P. July 11, 1997. "Real Boys Don't Read Books." *Times Education Supplement* no. 4228: A12–13.

Describes the impact of family background on literacy ability in boys, claiming that since promoting literacy is often regarded as the mother's role, it becomes difficult for boys to be both skilled in literacy and true to their understanding of how young males should act.

Gender-Fair Approaches to Literacy Learning: Strategies, Texts, and Curricula

Crawford, S. H. 1996. *Beyond Dolls and Guns: 101 Ways to Help Children Avoid Gender Bias.* Portsmouth, NH: Heinemann. ISBN 0-435-08129-2.

 Written specifically for parents, this useful book offers advice on how to identify bias in their child's environment; provides strategies for countering gender stereotyping; and suggests ways to teach children how to cope with the inequalities that they may encounter. Appendixes include a dictionary of nonsexist terminology, biographical sketches of famous women in history, and a list of gender-fair children's books.

Farmer, L. S. 1996. *Informing Young Women: Gender Equity Through Literacy Skills.* Jefferson, NC: McFarland. ISBN 0-786-40240-7.

 Farmer, a British librarian, offers an excellent and practical guide for promoting information literacy. The main focus is on helping teachers and librarians design gender-equitable projects, many of which extend beyond the classroom. Also included is a 151-item bibliography of resources.

Forrest, L. 1993. "Young Adult Fantasy and the Search for Gender-Fair Genres." *Journal of Youth Services in Libraries* 7 (fall): 37–42.

 Examines gender bias in young adult collections and suggests twenty-eight gender-fair fantasy titles.

Handy, A. E. 1996. "Gender Fairness Revisited: A Materials Update." *Book Report* 14 (January–February): 33–39.

 Focusing on junior high and high school readers, this useful annotated bibliography lists materials that contain high-quality representations of women. Most are nonfiction titles, but several fiction titles, videos, and CD-ROMs are included.

Hayn, J., and D. Sherrill. 1996. "Female Protagonists in Multicultural Young Adult Literature: Sources and Strategies." *The ALAN Review* 24 (1): 43–46.

 Offers a review of works with multicultural heroines plus points for discussion and study strategies.

Horgan, D. D. 1994. *Achieving Gender Equity: Strategies for the Classroom.* New York, NY: Allyn and Bacon. ISBN 0-20515-459X.

To ensure that present and future teachers are aware of the potential for gender inequity in their classrooms, Horgan offers practical strategies to address the issue.

Jenkins, C. A. 1993. "Young Adult Novels with Gay/Lesbian Characters and Themes, 1969–1992: A Historical Reading of Content, Gender, and Narrative Distance." *Journal of Youth Services in Libraries* 7 (fall): 43–55.

Librarians can be an invaluable aid in our search for gender-fair reading materials. This bibliography focuses on portrayals of gay and lesbian characters.

Kutenplon, D., and E. Olmstead. 1996. *Young Adult Fiction by African-American Writers, 1968–1993: A Critical and Annotated Guide.* New York: Garland. ISBN 0-81530-873-6.

This 432-page bibliography provides an important resource for young adult reading. It includes only fictional works written by or centering on African Americans.

Louie, A. 1993. "Growing Up Asian American: A Look at Some Recent Young Adult Novels." *Journal of Youth Services in Libraries* 6 (2) (winter): 115–127.

Reviews eight young adult novels about Asian Americans and concludes that all but one are stereotypical in their approach.

McCormick, T. M. 1994. *Creating the Nonsexist Classroom: A Multicultural Approach.* New York, NY: Teachers College Press. ISBN 0-8077-3348-2.

Urges teachers to recognize the sexist structure of education so that they can be agents of change. The book places a special emphasis on teacher education and offers guidelines for developing and implementing nonsexist curricula.

McKinney, C. S. 1996. "Finding the Words That Fit: The Second Story for Females in Young Adult Literature." *The ALAN Review* 24 (1): 11–14.

Focuses on critically acclaimed young adult novels from the last thirty years that provide excellent examples of strong females as they come of age; this complex passage is the "second story" to which the title refers.

Roberts, P., S. Alexander, and N. L. Cecil. 1993. *Gender Positive! A Teachers' and Librarians' Guide to Nonstereotypical Children's Literature, K–8.* Jefferson, NC: McFarland. ISBN 0-89950-816-2.

Recognizing the value of presenting children with literature in which characters break out of expected gender-role patterns, this work lists and discusses over two hundred such books and suggests target activities for each recommended book.

Stover, L. 1996. *Young Adult Literature: The Heart of the Middle School Curriculum.* Portsmouth, NH: Boynton/Cook Publishers. ISBN 0-86709-376-5.
　　Although it's without a specific gender focus, this book offers a guide for teachers who want to use young adult literature appropriately in the middle school classroom. It includes an excellent annotated list of YA titles.

Streitmatter, J. 1994. *Toward Gender Equity in the Classroom: Everyday Teachers' Beliefs and Practices.* Albany: State University of New York Press. ISBN 0-7914-1804-9.
　　Based on conversations with eight elementary and secondary school teachers, this book presents a variety of perspectives on the question of gender equity in the classroom. It highlights the differences between teachers' beliefs and practices; shows how institutions contribute to the formation of gendered identities; and offers suggestions for change. Part of SUNY's Teacher Preparation and Development series, edited by Alan R. Tom.

Vandell, K., and S. B. Dempsey. 1992. *Creating a Gender-Fair Multicultural Curriculum.* Washington, DC: American Association of University Women. ERIC, ED 371964.
　　Believing that the creation of a gender-fair multicultural curriculum is essential for equitable schooling, the authors present an overview of the national curriculum policy debate and offer concrete suggestions to ensure reform. They also offer advice about pitfalls that could damage the process.

Vandergrift, K. 1995. "Literacies of Inclusion: Feminism, Multiculturalism, and Youth." *Journal of Professional Studies* 3 (fall–winter): 39–47.
　　Looks closely at Canadian public school programs that are working toward encouraging literacy learning in a cultural inclusive and equitable way. Recommends supporting whole language programs and reader-response criticism.

Whaley, L., and L. Dodge. 1993. *Weaving in the Women: Transforming the High School English Curriculum.* Portsmouth, NH: Boynton/Cook Publishers. ISBN 0-86709-327-7.
　　This is a wonderful and lively discussion that compellingly answers the question "why study women?" and offers a rich and diverse selection of woman writers, along with practical ways to integrate their works into the cur-

riculum. Each chapter ends with an annotated list of further readings for students and resource books for teachers.

Adolescents, Gender, and Visual Literacy

Condron, L., and others. 1993. *Women and the Discourses of the Visual: Where Are Women in This Picture?* ERIC, ED 370583.

As increasing attention is paid to the importance of educating our students in visual literacy, we need to critically examine the gendered nature of visual representations. This document suggests that the social construction of women is very much tied to their visual-spatial representations.

Couch, R. A. 1995. *Gender Equity and Visual Literacy: Schools Can Help Change Perceptions.* ERIC, ED 380070.

Looks at visual representations of females in popular media as well as in textbooks and children's literature, and recommends specific changes that can work toward gender equity in the visual.

Damarin, S. K. 1993. "Ascendancy of the Visual and Issues of Gender: Equality Versus Difference." *Journal of Visual Literacy* 13 (fall): 61–71.

A useful overview of the differing ways males and females access media, how they are instructed in its use, and how they are portrayed by it.

Griffin, R. E., ed., and others. 1996. "VisionQuest: Journeys Toward Visual Literacy." Proceedings, International Visual Literacy Association Conference, Cheyenne, WY. October. ERIC, ED 408940.

Contains fifty-nine selected papers from the 1996 International Visual Literacy Association conference. While the focus is on visual literacy in general, several papers address issues such as gender equity online, gender and the media, and the intersection of gender and visual learning. Note especially "Out of the Picture, Out of the Club: Technology, Mass Media, Society, and Gender," by Nancy Nelson Knupfer and others.

Nentl, N., and R. J. Faber. 1996. "Where the Boys Are: Ad-Inspired Social Comparisons Among Male and Female Teens." Paper presented at the annual meeting of the Association for Education in Journalism and Mass Communication, Anaheim, CA, August 10–13. ERIC, ED 400572.

This fascinating study explores the degree to which adolescent males and females compare themselves to images from advertising. Of the more than 400 young men and women studied, girls were found to have a much higher incidence of negative comparison.

Adolescents, Gender, and Computer Literacy

Dresang, E. T. 1997. "Developing Student Voices on the Internet." *Book Links* 7 (September): 10–15.
Provides an annotated bibliography of young adult reading material that includes a 1997 list of Internet sites dealing with adolescent issues.

"Electronic School." 1997. *American School Board Journal* 184 (June): A1–A32.
An ASBJ supplement that provides hard-to-find information on software products targeted for girls, plus other news about the use of technology in schools in general and in reading programs specifically.

Hanson, W. R. 1994. "Student Drivers on the Information Highway." *Wilson Library Bulletin* 69 (November): 34–36.
This study of Internet use in a Canadian high school covers a wide variety of topics associated with online use, including gender bias in cyberspace.

Koch, M. 1994. "No Girls Allowed!" *TECHNOS* 3 (fall): 14–19.
Gender bias in the teaching of computer literacy has become an important issue for the next millennium. This article examines why girls are often discouraged in their use of computers and makes positive suggestions for change.

Mahoney, J., and N. N. Knupfer. 1997. "Language, Gender, and Cyberspace: Pulling the Old Stereotypes into New Territory." Paper presented at the annual convention of the Association for Educational Communications and Technology, Albuquerque, NM, February 14–18. ERIC, ED 409852.
Looks at how the social construction of gender is being replayed in cyberspace and shows how women avoid being stereotyped or harassed by using gender-neutral identification or restricting their activity to all-female user groups.

Nicholson, P. 1996. "From Web Master to Cyber Virgin: Girls' Explorations of the Internet." In *Schooling and Sexualities: Teaching for a Positive Sexuality.* Laskey, L., and C. Beavis, eds. Victoria, Australia: Deakin Centre for Education and Change.
Maintains that despite the caution that must be exercised by parents and teachers when letting young people explore it, the Internet does offer an opportunity to explore issues of gender, power, and sexuality.

Nye, E. 1991. "Computers and Gender: Noticing What Perpetuates Inequity." *English Journal* 80 (March): 94–96.

Reviews gender differences in computer learning styles and shows how software, curricula, and even classroom layout can affect how—and if—students become computer literate.

Additional Resources

This list is of organizations that have worked to design gender-balanced curricula, produce gender-balanced bibliographies, and host workshops. Because of problems related to funding and institutional commitment, organizations such as these often have a brief life span; all those listed below were operational as of January 1999.

American Association of University Women (AAUW)
111 16th Street NW
Washington, DC 20036
202/785-7700

Building Fairness Resource Center
Vocational Education Studies Department
Rehn Hall 135a
Southern Illinois University
Carbondale, IL 62901
618/453-3321, x241

Center for Research on Women
Wellesley College
106 Central Street
Wellesley, MA 02181
617/283-2500

Consortium for Educational Equity
Rutgers University
Building 4090 Livingston Campus
New Brunswick, NJ 08903
908/445-2071

Educational Equity Concepts
114 East 32nd Street, Suite 701
New York, NY 10016
212/725-1803

Girls Count
225 East 16th Avenue, Suite 475
Denver, CO 80203
303/832-6600

Girls Incorporated
National Resource Center
441 West Michigan Street
Indianapolis, MN 46202
800/374-4475
and
30 East 33rd Street, 7th floor
New York, NY 10016
212/689-3700

National Association for Women in Education
1325 18th Street NW, Suite 210
Washington, DC 20036
202/659-9330

National Coalition of Girls' Schools
228 Main Street
Concord, MA 01742
508/287-4485

National Women's Studies Association
University of Maryland
7100 Baltimore Avenue, Suite 301
College Park, MD 20740
301/403-0525

Racism and Sexism Resource Center for Educators
1841 Broadway
New York, NY 10023
212/757-5339

Women in Literature and Life Assembly of NCTE
1111 West Kenyon Road
Urbana, IL 61801-1096
800/369-6283

Women's Educational Equity Act Resource Center
Educational Development Center
55 Chapel Street
Newton, MA 02158
800/225-3088

Song of Happiness

Such was her happiness she held swift frogs
on their backs and stroked their patch of silver
belly like a pool of moon; the hazy gloss
on apples she enjoyed, but liked best the core,
to know the knotted seed was deep inside her
that could bear bloom, could bear light red and scent.
In the fall she went barefoot behind cows to stand
Ankle-deep in new shit, steaming soft,
to feel its slow heat moving up her legs, enough
to keep her body warm for that whole day.
Such was her happiness, her compost heap
became an orchard, and she bathed with fish
flitting aqua in the gorge so much
that sometimes at night while she dreamed
beneath the bright, and unnamed constellations,
fish swam from her ears, from out of her deepest sleep.
And when she woke on the round earth, rolling on her back
and she stood beneath that dome of blue,
damp grass on her clothes, her hair a mess,
She longed to make herself
closer to that blue, taller to that sky,
such was her happiness.

Jessica Jopp

About the Editors

Lynne Alvine is professor of English at Indiana University of Pennsylvania, where she directs the Southcentral Pennsylvania Writing Project, coordinates the Master of Arts in Teaching English program, and teaches graduate and undergraduate courses in English education. A middle school and high school English teacher for seventeen years, Lynne became a teacher educator in 1986. Her articles on adolescent literature and other topics related to English teaching have appeared in *The ALAN Review, SIGNAL, English Journal, WILLA,* and *High School Journal.* She has published chapters in the following books and reference collections: *Reclaiming the Classroom* (Heinemann Boynton / Cook), *Plain Talk: About Writing and Learning Across the Curriculum* (NCTE), *Adolescent Literature as Complement to the Classics, Vol. 2* (Christopher Gordon), *Identity Conflicts* (Greenwood), and *Writers for Young Adults* (Charles Scribner's Sons). A founding member of the Women in Literature and Life Assembly of NCTE, Lynne currently serves as chair of the NCTE Conference on English Education Commission on Gender Issues in English Teacher Education Programs.

Linda Cullum is a member of the composition faculty at West Chester University in West Chester, Pennsylvania. Her book reviews, bibliographies, and essays appear in such publications as *Library Journal, Notable Native Americans, WILLA,* and *MELUS,* the Journal of the Society for Multi-Ethnic Literature in the United States. She is also a frequent presenter at national writing conferences—speaking on such issues as the politics of identity construction; teaching and learning with the physically disabled; and service learning in the composition classroom.

About the Contributing Authors

Deborah Appleman is an associate professor, chair of the Educational Studies Department, and director of the Summer Writing Program at Carleton College in Northfield, Minnesota. Her research interests include adolescent response to literature, teaching literary theory to secondary students, and adolescent response to poetry. She has written widely on adolescent response to literature; is coeditor of *Braided Lives,* a multicultural literature anthology; and is currently writing a book on teaching literary theory to high school students.

Alice Cross, an English teacher at Horace Greeley High School in Chappaqua, New York, has written articles for *English Journal, Pittsburgh Magazine, Cineaste, WILLA,* and other periodicals.

Elizabeth Dutro is a doctoral candidate at the University of Michigan. Her research interests include gendered literacy practices, children's literature, and reader response. She is currently working with a group of fifth graders to explore how children negotiate gender in their reading of popular series fiction.

Andrea Fishman is an associate professor of English and director of the Pennsylvania Writing and Literature Projects at West Chester University. Her work on literacy and culture has appeared in *Language Arts, English Journal, English Education,* and *The Kappan.* She is the author of *Amish Literacy: What and How It Means* (Heinemann).

Judith Hayn is assistant professor of education in the Department of Curriculum and Teaching at Auburn University, where she directs the Sun Belt Writing Project and teaches courses in English education. Her research interests include adolescent literature and middle school education.

Jessica Jopp is a creative writer and instructor in the Department of English at Indiana University of Pennsylvania.

Kimra McPherson is an eleventh grader in Indiana, Pennsylvania. She has served as a correspondent for *Blue Jean* magazine and is active in the zining community.

Janet Montelaro is a research assistant professor in the Women's Studies Program and in the English Department at the University of Pittsburgh, where she teaches courses in feminist theory, women's literature, and children's literature. She is the author of *Producing a Womanist Text: The Maternal as Signifier in Alice Walker's The Color Purple* (1996 English Literary Studies Monograph Series). A teacher educator, she consults with area school districts in matters related to curriculum.

Annemarie Oldfield teaches English at University High School, an alternative high school in Roswell, New Mexico. A codirector and teacher consultant for the High Plains Writing Project, she is a specialist on incorporating writing into the curriculum and adapting curriculum for at-risk students.

Geraldine O'Neill, a French teacher who has retired from Horace Greeley High School in Chappaqua, New York, now works as an adjunct professor of foreign languages at Pace University. She has published in various educational journals.

Sara Rubinow is a former high school English and Spanish teacher. She currently resides in Boston, where she is studying industrial design.

Kathy Sanford is currently a teacher educator at the University of Alberta in Edmonton, Canada, after teaching in public schools for fifteen years. Her research interests include single-gender programs for girls and boys, elementary school gender issues, and alternative approaches to implementing and supervising teacher education programs.

Jennifer Sinor is a doctoral candidate in composition studies at the University of Michigan. Her interests also include women's autobiography and the ethics of representation. She is writing her dissertation on the diary of her great-great-great-aunt Annie, who was a homesteader in the Dakota Territories.

Lisa Spiegel, who has a special interest in rural education, is associate professor of curriculum and instruction at the University of South Dakota, where she teaches courses in adolescent literature and middle and secondary education. She is immediate past chair of the Women in Literature and Life Assembly of NCTE and serves on the executive committee of the Adolescent Literature Assembly of NCTE.

Lynn Spradlin is assistant professor of counseling and educational psychology at West Chester University of Pennsylvania, where she teaches courses in cross-cultural counseling, educational psychology, counseling techniques, and group processes. Her current research focuses on ways that race, social class, and gender stratification affect minority student achievement.